BREAK-OUT AT SIXTY-FIVE

BREAK-OUT AT SIXTY-FIVE

Tales of an Extraordinary Tourist

Cricket in the West Indies, Travels in Canada & China

by Percy J Salmon

NOMLAS
PRESS

Copyright © Percy J Salmon 2002
First published in 2002 by Nomlas Press
147 Pyrles Lane
Loughton, Essex IG10 2NH

Distributed by Gazelle Book Services Limited
Falcon House, Queen Square
Lancaster, England LA1 1RN

British Library Cataloguing in Publication Data
A catalogue record for this book is available from the British Library

ISBN 0-9540055-0-3

Typeset by Amolibros, Watchet, Somerset
This book production has been managed by Amolibros
Printed and bound by Advance Book Printing, Oxford, UK

Dedicated to all those whose company it has been my fortune to encounter.

Contents

List of Illustrations

Foreword
by
Peter Walker

Glamorgan & England cricketer

BBC commentator

Sitting under a palm leaf canopy at the edge of blemish-free white sand, sipping a rum punch cocktail from half a coconut and watching a setting sun gently turn the deep blue Indian ocean into ripples of orange, is not an environment conducive to saying "no" to anything!

So, when my travelling companion Percy Salmon with whom I'd shared the cricketing experience of a lifetime along with thirty other Gullivers Sports Travel clients watching England pull off an improbable Test Series victory in Sri Lanka, slipped into a neighbouring deck chair during four days of R&R in the Maldive Islands on the way home and asked if I would write a foreword to his proposed book, what else could I say but, "Yes."

Back in the UK, I inevitably gradually forget about this commitment. As a published author myself I knew just how long and arduous writing a full-length book can be and while I didn't doubt that Percy had some interesting stories to recall, for we'd shared some in Sri Lanka, I did wonder about his resolve. "I could write a book" is an oft-repeated cliché but rarely delivered, so not unnaturally I thought Percy, one of the more engaging characters on this planet, would fall into this category.

How pleasantly wrong I was. When his manuscript eventually arrived, some months later, it proved to be a gem!

Memorable moments worth recording are not just the preserve of the rich, the famous and the notorious for after reading his enthralling account of an anything but ordinary life you may feel that Percy Salmon deserves to be all three!

Percy shows an unerring eye for unusual detail coupled with that rare gift of being able to translate this into simple but vividly readable prose. From a visit to the Great Wall of China and a Royal Canadian Mounted police museum in Canada on to a near-death encounter with a tarantula spider in Trinidad, "Percy's world" is full of incident, anecdote and above all a feast of inter personal relationships; his verbatim recall of conversations adding immense colour to the moment.

Percy sat close to history in Antigua where he watched Brian Lara score his world record 375 in the fifth and final cricket Test against England in 1994 and it is his love of the summer game which fills many of the pages of his fascinating stroll through life.

Written in diary form, Percy Salmon, a latter-day Samuel Pepys, has left an indelible account of the twentieth century he lived in, where he never forgot to take time off to stop to smell the roses on the way.

Peter Walker
Cardiff
September 2001

A Chinese Introduction

2 5th February 1993, eleven-fifteen a.m., Gatwick to Beijing Air China Flight No 938, via Lucerne and Sharja airports, approx. flying time twelve hours.

This was by far my longest and highest altitude flight in an aircraft that I had ever experienced, just a routine one for some seasoned travellers, but to me, a first-timer, this would include a visit to one of the Wonders of the World, and possibly, in years to come (!), another in the making.

I had been told to take my camera with me and was excited with the knowledge of the prospect of using it as we crossed the roof of the world. There were several other snappers, who appeared from their conversation to be just as inexperienced as myself in making a photograph a lifelong memory. Those sitting near me were all of the same opinion: going East—what about the sun rising? "Not to worry, we'll find a way round that," the chap sitting opposite said. The time difference of eight hours did not have the slightest effect on me, for, as morning and a new dawn was breaking, I was wide awake watching the

Himalayas and the first sunbeams spread their tentacles far and wide below us. Nearly everyone was trying to locate a pane of glass which had not been badly mutilated, each armed with a camera at the ready, so I joined them first on one side of the aircraft and then the other. What photographs these were going to turn out to be!

Below, and all around us on either side of the wings, was a sight that is going to be a formidable commission to describe. Clouds in their strange shapes and sizes, now tinged with orange, purple, and golds, were rolling and wandering away into obscurity, and every now and again a black or brown coloured cone of no particular formation put in an appearance through this wool-gathering community, topped with a more distinctive shade of white. I found myself holding my breath! *"Snow-capped peaks!"* An eerie silence followed for a short while as a numbness took over my whole being.

"Did you see the size of that one?" a passenger shouted in my ear. What she was pointing at was an extra large peak, which to me seemed to broadcast its message across this whole sacrosanct kingdom: "I am one of the chief warden protectors!" The spell had been broken!

Beijing, twelve-twenty, only a few minutes from our scheduled time of arrival, and coming into land I remarked how quiet it appeared to be, not many people about or aircraft for that matter. I was politely told this is the dormancy period for travel here, most everyone taking a beverage!

We were to be met by Peter who was to be our tour manager. He had a group visa for us all, so nobody could move without it. In this period of waiting in the customs area, I became quite interested in a particular room opposite. Police and army personnel kept coming and going in a never-ending stream. Wandering over for a closer inspection, I saw that each individual had a glass jar, with something like string forming a handle. Why, of course, it was *tea!* I must say it did look a most intimidating *cuppa*. The comrades sat down to quaff this liquid, no doubt discuss the foreigners outside, and then depart. This tea looked thoroughly unpleasant with all the ullage abounding! In days to come, I would be partaking of many such cups with Chinese people of all walks of life, but I'm glad to say not with quite so many foreign bodies.

Peter had now arrived, just as we were all beginning to despair of what might have happened to him. He was a bright and breezy type, and "no problem", his pet phrase, cheered us up no end. The journey to our hotel took the best part of three-quarters of an hour as traffic on the road was very busy. I have seen cambers on French roads, but this made you want to move to the centre of the bus for safety. Alongside us for most of the journey was a new motorway clearly under construction, heading into the city. It appeared hooters were almost as important as traffic lights, as our driver, Mr Shrew, was constantly making use of his. Arriving at our hotel, Peter informed us, "Anyone who would like to go to the Forbidden City and Tian an Men Square should be ready in one and a half hours. Dinner will be at seven-thirty p.m."

I settled for a siesta. In my room on the table, I found two large silver containers, both with large cork stoppers. They were thermos-lined, one for tea, one for hot water, and the appropriate necessities nearby. This was very welcoming and very sustaining. What was rather unique at our evening meal, and all subsequent meals with four or more people sitting, was the table we sat round. It was circular with the centre part revolving, with all the edibles and light refreshment placed so you could stop the table, reach across and help yourself to whatever you wanted.

Good friendly atmospheres abounded, especially between a high-profile lawyer, John, and myself, who quite often would say, "Have you got your beer, Percy?" A quick move on the roulette wheel and there it was, gone—certainly something different from our own restaurant tables! As to the meals, I would say that what you were presented with at lunchtime, you almost certainly received for dinner. Chopsticks were optional; most of us tried these at the start of meals, but none of us became accomplished. After our meal a few of us decided on an evening stroll. We had been assured by Peter that this was the safest city in the world to move in; unspeakable and untellable recriminations would occur if any foreigners were to come to any harm.

Early morning, a familiar noise was to wake me up regularly, phut, phut, phut, phut. I had not a clue what it might be and it was always forgotten as the day's programme unfolded.

This day would be one I had waited for nearly all my working life, never really daring to believe I would stand or even walk on it—of course The Great Wall of China. First of all, on our journey to Ba Da Ling, we stopped off at a Friendship store, selling everything in the way of gifts and souvenirs, plus huge oriental vases. On arrival at the Great Wall, which we have seen continuously through our bus windows for several miles, Peter tells us we can either turn right which is quite an easy route, or to the left, which is more difficult. One could see in the distance a quite sharp climb to a faraway turret.

As we climbed the steps, we seemed to be besieged by locals who were on parade selling everything from flags, caps, handkerchiefs and scarves all brightly coloured. The wall was twenty-two feet high, some twelve feet wide with observation battlements some four feet high that made a safe walkway but did not protect against the cold wind. I had asked Peter that as visiting this place had been a long-term ambition of mine, could I stop here all day and perhaps he could pick me up later? "Certainly not, out of the question, as we're on a tight schedule, and due to take lunch at one p.m. at the eating place nearby. You're all to be back here within one and a half hours." So I decided to tackle the hard section and found all of my companions were doing the same. This headed towards the western hills in the distance as far as the eye could see, like a giant caterpillar threading its way through distant mountain ranges.

The wall was built from a type of granite, the paved walkways and gentle gradients, all in the same material with the steps formed from stone similar to Yorkshire paving. It was restored here by the Ming Dynasty some 500 years ago.

My companions and I could see in the distance rather a steep climb with an observation turret at the top. Indeed it was, as we approached we saw it was about thirty feet in length, but the climb I should say was one in two. A brass rail was a major help up and down. On my microcassette recorder, where I am talking into the mike, I sound as if I had walked several miles. Reaching the top, the turret had stood out like a Belisha beacon for some distance. You could look out and wonder at this marvellous construction, the work involved, the hardship that must have been an everyday experience, and the lives that were shovelled into oblivion for every foot of its length, which is far in excess of the 2,484 miles documented. It would have made my day if I had witnessed workmen repairing it, but that was not to be.

It did not matter if you hid behind a column to avoid the sellers or trades-people, they found you as soon as you showed your face. One chap, after I had left the turret to come down, never left me for several hundred yards; he was trying to sell me a certificate or suchlike. Down the steep section, either just in front or at the side, I was glad the rail was there, for he was behaving like the proverbial mountain goat. Here he was joined by others all offering the same sort of business transaction. My companions were all receiving the same treatment. I dived into my pocket and found about forty fens (100 make up one yuan). I thrust this into his hand telling him to go away. I will not forget his face for a long time, (a typical ruddy-faced Chinese), for it lit up, transforming his features. Saying something to his companions (I suppose he thought the good spirit had returned in the guise of a foreigner), he offered his hand in friendship, which I accepted, for he had not parted with any paperwork.

When we walked down the steps, we all remarked how the wall was so consistent with the sometimes extraordinary gradients that it passed over. Looking over the easy section, you could see the workmen would have made good progress with that section. But again all materials had been carted, as Peter had told us, from miles away. He also told us that some parts of the Great Wall had provided new homes with bricks and stones, the latter having been removed from it without breaking any bylaws as regards thieving, trespassing, breaking and entering. He was asked if there were any "regulations" to preserve this wonderful treasure. "There are none in some parts," he replied. I explained to him that if this continued there would not be a Great Wall in the centuries to come, but he just shrugged his shoulders.

Now don't get me wrong, Peter, I can assure you was a very intelligent Chinaman, having spent several years in America, and knowing a lot more about foreign policies, yes even our own, than us, his visitors. When he was asked at one stage about China as a trading nation in future years, he was most emphatic about the situation, saying that China, perhaps before the year 2000 would be Far East No 1. How about Japan? He said very definitely that Japan was a pushover - no problem!

After this very short visit, which was accomplished in bitterly cold temperatures, the wind hardly ceasing and all the mountain streams frozen solid, we made our way back to Beijing.

That afternoon was going to take us to two places of exceptional interest, both hundreds of years apart, but both enabling you to familiarise yourself with past and present. What the various dynasties enjoyed in their lifetime all those years ago!

The approach to the Ming Tombs is very impressive. The road takes you past eighteen pairs of animals, perhaps more—lions, camels, elephants, horses and mythical creatures, each one being carved from a single rock, also a huge stone gallery with carved archways, known as "The Spiritway". Peter told us that the tomb's site was originally encircled with a wall, which was now long gone.

The most important tomb belonged to the Third Ming Emperor, who was responsible for building much of Peking, now Beijing. His tumulus is marked by a steel tower and is known as "The Precious Fortress". So far, it has not yet been disturbed. We went inside the Hall of Sacrifice; it was built in 1427 and is supported by thirty-two pillars made of Nawmu wood beams, purlins, rafters and brackets from south-west China. I can honestly say this is another place where you hold your breath and talk just above a whisper. The columns are just perfect, no damage, no trace of any disfigurement, no disease and no woodworm. They seemed almost machine-made. It took six years to complete this building, but what a wonderful example it is of hardwood perfection.

The next tomb was of the Emperor Wawli, 1573-1620. It was excavated in 1958. When they opened it all up, it was found to be crammed with about three hundred assorted garments, all obviously for the emperor's use in the nether world. Beside these, there were countless pieces of jewellery, curios and porcelain, stowed in twenty-six lacquered chests. What a life of Riley the emperor would have looked forward to! In the area behind the tomb, are three apartments, two contain articles of use at the time of his departure, the other one is empty. Peter told us, "This is empty for it awaits the emperor's return."

All credit to the surroundings, for the paintwork is in excellent condition and typified everything about the Ming Dynasty 1368-1644.

This was to be a lasting impression as my travels progressed—the quality of the wood, stonework, the corbelling of a number of buildings here had to be seen to believed. To enjoy the magnitude of these structures, it was clearly the architect's view that only the very best material was used to make sure preservation was paramount. The exhibition halls outside, the regalia and treasures were there for us all to observe and wonder at.

Moving back into Beijing, we visited the jade factory, which employed 1,700 people. Up a lift to the seventh floor, then we came down gradually, visiting each floor in turn, each having a different task. The penultimate one really caught my attention; the pottery vases had been made, both large and small, and now the intricate artwork was being applied. Very fine copper strands were used in making patterns of all descriptions around the vase. I asked Peter if he could ask the Chinese lady how long she had been doing this and the answer was twenty years. I asked, "Surely not on the same bench?"

"Yes, the same one," was the reply.

I told Peter this would not occur in England, the trade unions would not allow this, after two days there would be a change around. Peter told her this, but the reply was a quiet shrug of her shoulders and a weak smile.

Sunday meant a six a.m. start, for we were to take an optional trip to Chendge in north-east China, a trip of 155 miles, taking some five hours. First to Beijing railway station, up the concrete steps into the main hall, and there were bodies, hundreds upon hundreds of them, lying all over the place, all alive, and seemingly contented– blankets, bags, sacks, children dressed in every colour you could possible think of. Peter told us to keep close together and watch our luggage. After half an hour he came back from the ticket office, "No problem." We then walked single-file down through this crazy maze to find a diesel loco pulling some fourteen carriages. At seven a.m. there came a shrill whistle and we were on our way. The first part of our journey was quite uneventful with cups of tea at two yuan, approximately twenty-five pence, quite enjoyable. The scenery soon changed, quite dramatically in fact–lakes and rivers both sides of the carriage, all frozen over with mountains and glaciers in the distance. Peter, our guide, was with six other tour managers who were having a short vacation to Chendge not having been there before, and so we would be handed over to another guide.

We arrived at the Orange Hotel just after noon to find Mr Bi (pronounced Mr B) would be our guide for the next couple of days. He was one of the old school, brown jacket, blue trousers and black peaked cap in his pocket at the ready. The tour bus took us across quite a large river, frozen solid with no water running at all, to our very modern hotel. After a spruce-up, our table was, as usual, the circular type, loaded with goodies. The afternoon was, I would say, an educational one, as just outside Chendge was a silk factory. It appeared from the outside just an ordinary factory, one with two floors, and other buildings all much smaller. On entering, we all realised how far behind China is with regard to working conditions, for they seemed to be early Victorian methods. The factory employed 2,000 people, seventy-five per cent of whom were women of widely different ages, some as young as twelve years old.

The first floor contained silk that was made up, patterns completed and designers busy working on new designs, with the busy chatter of machines, which I presumed were driven by steam from some part of the building. A huge table caught your eye instantly; several Chinese ladies were seated, sorting out the silk cocoons into three grades, good, medium and low. They were then dipped into temperatures approaching 112 degrees centigrade and then transferred to various length and size spools. Colouring also took place with this operation, one girl operating each machine, sitting on an iron-framed seat with a soft cushion, fixed on rails that had a sideways motion only travelling about five feet, but it enabled the operator to move quickly and efficiently. We were allowed to take photos here, the authorities not being concerned about the conditions. An example then, of how strong silk is, was shown to us by two white-coated officials. One held the end of the silk while the other walked with a spool in his hand the whole length of the building, perhaps a hundred feet, holding it about his head. Both appeared to be pulling on it, but it held firm. Mind you, you had to have good eyesight to observe this, but seeing is believing and I was one of the believers! Finally, we went into the sales department where all those finished articles of silk were paraded for us all to wonder at. Then you had to place one hand firmly on your tempting wallet.

1st March—Mr Bi arrived early, and as I found that I had a cold developing, I asked him what medicine I should purchase. He called me "Percee", and said after our day's business he would get some treatment for me. The kindergarten visit was first, about four different tours arrived at this small hillside school, where we found not only day pupils but also boarding ones as well. This was the first day back after Xmas, and Jean, our learned lady, said it was remarkable how organised they were on the first day back at school. Aged from two to five, you can imagine they were resplendent in their gaily coloured clothing. First of all some thirty people packed into the classroom. There was a Chinese welcome of much bowing, then several songs accompanied by a teacher on a very ancient harmonium. There followed a game of musical chairs, recitations, then musical chairs for the foreign visitors and finally everybody joined in, with several youngsters very interested in my camera and the pictures I was taking. Mr Bi told me they were calling me granddad. Then we visited the sleeping quarters, each bed you saw reminding me of the cake and bread trays that you see when you visit Sprays our local baker, but these had legs on. All the children seemed very happy and contented.

The rest of this very bright, very cold day was a visit to the Emperor's mountain resort. I will try to be as brief as possible in describing this explosion of perfection as it truly is mind-boggling - 5,640,000 square metres with 384 buildings all scattered around in the shape of a crescent moon. On the north and east sides are twelve magnificent temples all representing different styles of ethnic nationalities including Yan, Tibetan and Mongolian. The temples are all built outside the old capital, eight of them known as the outer temples and administered by lamas. The whole area is enclosed by a wall, built with material comparable to what we had seen at The Great Wall—some twenty feet high, perhaps ten feet wide and again with battlements and look-out turrets like the Great Wall. What I did notice as we moved around, presuming it was all original, was how it had kept its natural appearance, lakes, steep gradients, small coppices, the hills, rocks, large and small. The buildings that came upon you so suddenly seemed to have appropriate names that suited what you might be enjoying and admiring–Pavilion of Refreshing Music, Hall of Quiet Waters and Cloudy Hills, Pavilion of Fragrant Isle, Mountain Abode of Tranquil Comfort, Hall of Warning Against Gains, Temple of Gathering Spring were just a few of the buildings we were to see, enjoy, marvel at and feel fulfilled by in the next few hours.

In the Dynasty period, within twelve months of a decision being made with regard to a birthday, an anniversary, whatever took the Emperor's fancy, or was suggested to him, the area was selected and the building up and working. The workforce would have had to be without a shadow of doubt, all qualified artists, as each and every part of each building is a work of art. Even the very low-grade labourer must have been awarded an accolade on completion. I suppose it was most important what the emperor was, a kind one or a tyrant. Mr Bi said many were the latter.

The Emperor's Palace, The Ching Dynasty (1644-1911)

Here there were paintings, chiefly of hunting in the grounds, all sorts of animals including tigers, and all sadly in need of a good wash and brush up. I mentioned this to Mr Bi who said, "No, not touched, the portraits better if looking old and ancient." Well they were certainly that.

In the palace grounds was the Hall of Frugality and Sincerity. It was here in 1877 that a high-ranking officer of a foreign country refused to bow to the emperor. Around this area was a wealth of history as Mr Bi enthused over telling us just a fragment of its life through time. If one of the emperors came here for perhaps six months at a time, he would be carried all the way from Peking, the old capital, taking fifteen days, so fifteen palaces were built along the way for him to take his rests. We asked Mr Bi if he was a tall or short person. "Not quite sure," he replied. "One metre and some millimetres," which had us all in fits of laughter. But on the serious side, if there was an accident and he was accidentally tipped from the carriage, perhaps six carriers all would have unmentionable things done to them, then finally - chop, chop!

One of the rooms we looked in was a reading room, used by the emperor's relations when they came to visit him. When you think that just one emperor had eighty concubines, he must have had quite a few relations. Gambling and smoking seemed to have been the most popular pastime. Another rather unusual room was a beauty parlour of days long gone. Mr Bi explained that most parts of China had them—where the gentry had daughters with ambition, then here was the place where they would spend a lot of that life. Beauty treatment was not as we know it, facial attention, etc., but emphasis was on the feet, most important from the age of three and four. Young girls would have their feet embalmed, so as to make sure they did not grow. They would very seldom leave such places as this until suitors were found for them at the age of fifteen, sixteen and seventeen, then the smaller the feet the better the reward of wealth.

As we walked round, obviously we could not understand the writing, but Mr Bi pointed out that when writing was started over 1,000 years ago, you had to read downwards. We asked him if he could read a piece like this and translate it into English so that we could all understand. He did this admirably and we all clapped, which I am sure made his day. Now and again, we came across tapestries, or drawings that you could more easily follow.

Moving into the lake area, another temple caught your eye, Hui, Wan, Zong, Chun, Zhio, Miad (The Temple of Gathering Spring). This first day of March was very bright and cold, but cheerful, and it's difficult for one to ascertain what spring would look like. But today my quick observation: trees all bare, everywhere cold and without life, the odd robin nervously heralding a welcome to us all with a very weak note if it was one.

My own imagination often relays to me what sort of scene we could expect to appreciate if it was any of the other three seasons. I suppose that with these conditions prevailing, my mind was a blank. I drew Mr Bi's attention to this situation, who quickly explained that the change is quite dramatic here. All around us is transformed in the spring by pear, plum, peach blossoms, with the whole locality coming alive through a combination of musical melodies, from countless numbers of birds and frogs busy with their own musical arrangements. As the summer arrives, red, pink and white lotus flowers appear and abound on the lake together with water-lilies, again with various colour schemes, and then as Mr Bi so eloquently tells us, "These all create the softest of ripples on the lake's surface, which in turn form a silent arrangement of music that you could only wish to imagine."

Mr Bi continues, having seen this so many times, "The autumn colourings are the most spectacular with the various cultivars of acers and aspens, which are all around us, each one trying its hardest to outperform the neighbouring tree or shrub." He had a voice that made you want to listen to him and from his knowledgeable portrayal of this scene a lasting image was certainly imprinted in my grey cells.

The lake area is divided into eight lakes of various sizes, the Ruyi island is the largest one. It resembles the S-shape jade ornament, Ruyi. When the total area with all its connecting bridges and islands was originally mapped out, I can only imagine the satisfaction this must have given the landscape architect on completion. Mr Bi tells us the ice is one metre thick, while almost everyone is slipping and sliding, falling over and moving around to try to keep the cold out. We had noticed several old rowing boats that were lying along the edges of the lake. "Yes, some of them are over fifty years old, and in the summer months they're loaded down like our buses." They reminded me of my youth and the ones we used to see on Connaught Water.

Back at the hotel, Mr Bi was as good as his word, saying, "You come with me, Percee."

Just around the corner were dozens of bicycles chained up to trees, railings or whatever. As Mr Bi unlocked his, padlocked back and front, I remarked how unsafe it appeared to be—no I was not to worry, very safe, no problem. Walking along he told me a little about himself. Both his parents were professors of medicine in a rural part of China, and yes, he had followed this calling too, and was able to write out prescriptions for most ailments. A few years ago, realising that he could earn a lot more yuan by being a tour manager, he decided against all forms of medicine.

Reaching a parade of shops, that from the outside looked like repair shops, dismal and dark with paint peeling off everything you looked at, we go in. Facing us is a counter some ten foot long and about two foot wide. Mr

Bi talks to the supervisor handing him the prescription he had made out for me. The medicines arrive, and I duly handed over the eleven yuan (approximately £1.30) required. Outside Mr Bi tells me how I should take the medicine and pills, telling me also that medical care is available to most Chinese every day of every week (this is free of course), between six and nine p.m. "End-of-street surgeries take place; in fact, if you look over there you will see a queue starting to form."

Telling me how I was to get back to my hotel, and then with a "See you in the morning" he joined the multitude of cyclists heading home.

I had found out more about some of the bicycles earlier in the day. Some of them are towing trailers; if laden with rubbish, then each one is either going or coming back from a council depot—by rubbish I mean anything recyclable: tins, paper, plastic, even wood. You really need to witness some of those loads, not only a trailer load, but usually another huge one on the cyclist's back. It appears that it is all worthwhile as they are paid for this service.

Most of the sensible people cycling or walking were wearing a form of butter muslin across their mouth and nose. This had two purposes—guarding against pollution or the flu.

Reaching a major junction that I had to cross, as I was on foot I decided I would go the long way round. Otherwise, quite literally in crossing, you had to have your head revolving like their restaurant tables. Going round was certainly going to be a healthy way of living longer! Chinese were still on the roadside selling all sorts of vegetables and fruit. Bicycle repairers are quite frequent to the eye. It seems at every fourth aspen tree there is a business concern. A traffic policeman has a blue uniform, white gloves. He certainly has his work cut out as four very wide roads meet here. His pillbox is raised off the ground with a single red and white chequered pole that turns at right angles just above his head to support the roof. Inserted in the roof on all four sides are rows of different coloured lights, very much in control.

Back at the hotel, a welcome cuppa, marvellous! Then I took my medicine. It was revolting stuff, the pills not too bad, though. I told Mr Bi this in the morning and he said, "You soon be much better, Percee."

Again, a fascinating day was in store for us, this time to the emperor's summer mountain resort. The buildings are all maintained by lamas, and chiefly built in styles very similar to the ones we had seen yesterday, but perhaps these were more distinctive with their intricate top dressing! Flowing hips and ridges, wonderful dragons and other creatures, golds, blues and purples to name just a few. I will try to describe one of the many temples, the Temple of Universal Peace. It has a huge statue of Guynin inside, (the Goddess of Mercy). She has a thousand arms and a thousand eyes, and to me she was utterly perfect. Whatever sculpture was made and put on this earth to be scrutinised, this is the one that takes the biscuit, for all around you there existed this feeling of mercy and forgiveness. The Temple is 36.75 metres high, and there was very little between the roof and her top piece, so this gives you an idea of what I was observing. (It would have been a perfect solution to have a mechanical lift to gently take you up and down to see every piece in detail.) Even now, as I describe it, I cannot remotely do justice to this awesome but sympathetic figure.

It is made from a very hard wood; it could well have been the Nawmu wood used at the Hall of Sacrifice at Beijing. If so, this one varied in that it was highly varnished, and glistened. Mr Bi tells us this is a model of the one in Tibet and this one weighs 110 tons, and is supposedly the biggest in the world. What a masterpiece of carving! I have seen many sculptured wood carvings, ceilings, walls and even large pieces of furniture but this was different. It did not matter where I looked, to me everything seemed faultless. Jean tells me that each finger and thumb has a different implication. I might add here that she appears to be a very learned lady and a well travelled one as well for many years, and I feel sure she is not at all embarrassed when Mr Bi refers to her as the professor. When you think that one thousand arms are attached, and every single finger means something different—yes each finger and thumb is shaped to a distinct meaning, good luck, good fortune, illness, fate etc.—this is quite extraordinary. There are lots more but I certainly can only remember those I have mentioned, and just look how many ways just one of them could be interpreted, as Jean wisely pointed out at the time.

Outside there is another large temple, this one quite a way up the fairly steep hillside. The approach looked quite formidable. Mr Bi said if we wanted to go up and take some pictures, we only had twenty minutes. The treads and risers that formed the steps had been cut out of the mountain stone, and all were very irregular, colour and texture like Cumberland stone.

At the top of the hill, we had come through a dense patch of gorse bushes. This in itself made our journey up worthwhile, each of us busy snapping away, taking in views of the temples around us and in the far distance to our left a local landmark, The Sledge Hammer Peak. This, together with one called The Frog Peak, had remarkable likenesses from where we stood. Mr Bi had said it was difficult to come down, and, my, it was, for it was testing the knee operation I had had some three months previously to the limits.

Our final temple was on the other side of Chendge, the Temple of Heaven and quite appropriately built on the Hill of Heaven. Winding roads and S-bends took us to this marvel at the summit. It was a huge temple, which only had the one pantiled roof of a deep red colour, and while we were looking round, in and out, a drawback became apparent; you had to climb fifty steps to get to the top part. The delightful lama's music was being played the whole time; it never stopped, so I took the chance to record this enchanting music. I found a wide area with a nice sensible 3,000-feet-high parapet wall and it was here I sat down and wound the tape back to listen to the recording of the melodies belting out not only from up and around us but now my recording too. Mr Bi was quickly on the scene, and just as quickly wanted to offer me a considerable amount of yuan for the purchase of the machine. We sat on top of the wall, and he offered me up to two hundred yuan—no doubt a lot of money to him—but as I had paid nearly fifty pounds less than year ago, and was very pleased with it, I was certainly not going to part with it. He could see that I was not interested in doing a deal, but I used the opportunity of a quiet moment with him to ask him about the boats we had seen yesterday.

So I asked, "Mr Bi, did those boats we saw on Lake Ruyi really have passengers crowded on them like your buses?"

I recall his expression, quite well, of amazement. "Percee, if the boat capacity says ten you can be sure there is twenty on the boat." I told this to one or two of the others later, but as none had been here before who could disagree?

I took a few more photos of the superb views across the valleys that lay round us on three sides of the Temple. Coming down again to terra firma was pretty daunting, and I was certainly glad to arrive at the bottom, taking a quick walk around what I thought was probably a terrific garden in the summer months. It was all laid out in neat enclosures surrounded with low box hedging about one foot high. This finalised our visit to the Temple of Heaven.

Back to the hotel and already packed, we all said our goodbyes to Mr Bi, thanking him for his excellent interpretations and I told him I would come again sometime, but I wasn't really sure I would.

The train left for Beijing at two p.m., some twelve carriages attached to the one diesel locomotive. Again, the carriage allocated to us was clean and tidy with a pleasant smell of some sort. For the whole of the journey back, the cheerful Chinese stewardess was very attentive, wanting to sell us something throughout the journey. Mr Bi had warned us, as Peter had done, of the Chinese-style lavatory system. He said if the train was swaying about, and one was not practised, not to use them. Having investigated this, you could understand why! Back in the carriage it was not long before I decided that I should take more photos as perhaps those I had snapped coming up might not have been successful. A Chinese couple sitting directly opposite me were quite amused at my method of taking photos. We were soon chatting away and having a good look at my camera. They remarked that it was not a very expensive one, and did I expect to get photos through the double-glazed windows? "Yes," I replied, "I feel quite sure that they will be first class," but I really had had doubts in my mind since coming over on the jumbo jet. They wished me luck anyway.

After about an hour my knee joint was getting quite painful, so I decided to walk through the carriages. I was doing this as the train was passing through a series of S-bends. I looked out one side to see the front part of the engine going into a mountain tunnel. Moving across to the other side, I saw the rear ones in the opposite direction and seeing this I realised that Chinese carriages are much longer than our own at home. When I got back, tea had arrived, so I decided to see if this might refresh parts that other tipples do not reach! My newfound friends, Jane and Jim, and myself were now on first-name terms, and they told me they lived in Singapore and he was the station-master there. Any time I was in the area I was to look them both up. We were talking about how to handle chopsticks, which I admitted I found most difficult to use as against our knife and fork. Jim explained that it was quite easy, so, diving in my holdall, I found a pair, which had accidentally dropped in, and screwing up some pieces of paper, I asked him to demonstrate very quickly. He soon proved how accomplished he was, picking up those pieces again and again. I tried and told him that if the pieces were thicker and more substantial I thought I would succeed, so I screwed all the pieces into quite a large ball of paper, which I then carefully picked up, only to drop it at the point of entry.

It was now totally dark. Peter our guide was now back

with us telling us that we were about half an hour late and dinner would be at eight p.m. sharp. He asked me if I was all right as I appeared to be limping. I replied that I doubted if I would be able to make the flight tomorrow for Xian. "Oh yes, you will, they have a clinic in the hotel," he replied. I mentioned that now we had arrived at Beijing railway station that there seemed to be more people than before. He answered that they had come here to sleep as it was warmer here.

Back at the hotel, I asked the manageress about the clinic and my knee; she replied it was all closed up for the night, but they would send me to the hospital, as I had to be up early in the morning. So after a quick wash and brush up, followed by a light snack, I was on my way to the hospital by eight-thirty p.m. in the charge of a very good Chinese, Billy, one of the porters, who was to look after me. He spoke reasonably good English and explained that he was a supporter of Tottenham Football Club. I told him he was in good company as I was one too. The taxi was a private one and I was to pay when I had finished using it.

Well, anybody would think, the way we were driving through Beijing, that my life was slowly ebbing away, as corners were almost being taken on two wheels. We arrived at the gates, only to find that this, the main entrance, was closed for the night and we had to go to the rear entrance—more brake screeching and horns blaring. Getting out of the taxi I asked Billy, "Where's the hospital?" "Follow me," he replied. Everywhere was in total darkness; as my eyes got used to where Billy was leading me, I saw a small cabin directly on the left, from where an attendant led us and let us into the main part of the building. Lighting was at a minimum as we moved from corridor to corridor; only one lamp at each end was alight. Billy explained this was a very old hospital; the new one would be ready next year. For those who can remember the old workhouse at St Margaret's, the colour scheme was identical! Brown and cream! Then one long corridor, about three cricket pitches long with, at the far end, an illuminated sign - FOREIGN VISITORS CLINIC. By this time, Billy was supporting me with one arm and I suppose it looked quite bad to the white-coated doctor on duty. I tried in vain, through Billy, to say that I had had an arithroscopy knee operation. After an examination, he said he wanted x-rays, then told Billy where we were to go—up several flights of stairs and along a couple of corridors all with the same sort of non-existent lighting, but I could not have cared less, so long as I could have my knee improved somehow. The Chinese who did the x-rays must have been busy, as we had to wait something like thirty minutes before he saw us. He took two pictures, one on one side and one on the other. I watched them being developed and removed from a green forty-gallon water tank, and then, dripping wet, he placed them in a large envelope and handed them to Billy.

Down on the ground floor again, the doctor said, via Billy, that there was no fracture, no break, no bones broken or out of place. As Billy had no doubt told him that we were being awakened at five-thirty in the morning for our flight to Xian to see the Terracotta Warriors, he said he would make me better and I would not miss the flight. He gave Billy a prescription telling us to collect the medicines from the hospital pharmacy. Billy did call it something but what I cannot recall. We went through the corridor and came to a nine inch by six inch aperture with a metal hatch about four foot six inches from the floor. Billy tapped on this, and a hand came through and took the prescription. We waited five minutes, but the account had to be settled first, otherwise no medicine. I gave the twenty-two yuan to Billy who handed it in. Talk about that song: "And lightning fast was he"! This Chinaman, whether male or female was quick, and the shutter even quicker. The medicine duly arrived. I thanked them in English, but could see no person, only the hand, and then it was - gone.

The taxi driver had been very patient, the time now eleven-thirty as we arrived back at the hotel. Billy said twenty-seven yuan, just under £3.50, but I gave him thirty. He was very pleased. No, I did not want a receipt. "Yes," Billy says. "Most important you take accounted receipt." He gave me instructions how to take the pills, the medicine and yes, musk and tiger balm, the latter in the form of a poultice, like a very thin slice of toast. I was to place this under and over my knee. Fortunately, I had brought my elastic bandage, which was quite long for it went from almost mid-thigh to my ankle. This I carefully slipped on. It was midnight. I was soon awakened by the phut, phut, phut long before dawn was breaking, then the call on the bedroom phone, bang on time.

Quick breakfast, cereals, toast or whatever, all our party ready and packing for the two days is quickly completed. As my companions could see, my knee was much better. The pain had gone, and I told them what cure I had received and how I'd placed it on the offending part. I had to show them samples of this very ancient healing treatment. The cold was no better though.

The North West China Airline flight to Xian (pronounced Sian) took a little over two hours. We were met by a charming Chinese lady Ms Lee, who gave us a good insight into this very old city as we drove to our hotel. I must say we were all impressed by her wit and intelligence. She had studied in America with her brother for several years, and appeared, like Peter, to have a wealth of knowledge.

On the journey, which took perhaps half an hour, we passed several mounds of earth. She explained that each one belonged to various emperors of dynasties over the centuries, but to us this was unique, so we asked why care was not taken of them—they were just large mounds with a few shrubs or bushes growing there. There appeared to be no sign of a tombstone or any dedication. "Perhaps one day," Lee says.

Over lunch, this time served up in the Orange Hotel on ultra-modern circular glass tables, including a centrepiece—usual menu. The afternoon: we went right back in time, in fact to the Neolithic Village of Banpo, 6,000 years old. It was discovered in 1953. The whole area was excavated and now put on show for us. There is a replica life-size building of the original; it would have been at ground level at that time, but it is now dug out to represent how it would have looked—a cone-shaped building consisting of four wood posts around the centre supporting the roof, partition walls and external ones, covered with mud and straw. The building is a fair size as it covers thirty square metres. It has a hole in the roof so smoke can get away from the sunken hearth, which is just offset from the supports. Lee told us that these people invented steam cookers. We were all agog about this—what on earth would they have used a steam cooker for? Very convincingly, she assured us they steamed bread; who were we to disagree? There are two museum wings at the front of the Banpo enclosure; one contains an oil painting illustrating how the village went about its business all those years ago—yes, even a cemetery for the departed. We also saw picture-writing examples on some of the pottery that had been found while the excavation was in progress. The pottery is made, it appears, from a very fine red clay. Not only pieces, but whole specimens have been found. Finally, we went into the showpiece itself; inside, modern potters were busy, with young artists finishing the articles, so displaying their talents. All shapes and sizes of pots and jugs were receiving enthusiastic attention.

Then Xian itself: we were now to look at another pagoda-type building that we had seen from a fair distance, soaring skywards with majestic aplomb. We had parked up and now as we reached this towering construction, we saw that it was built on top of the Wall that almost surrounds Xian and that in itself is eight and a half miles long (or fourteen kilometres). We had now climbed up to the top of the wall, and—just to give you an idea of the size of the area we were standing on—at the base the width is fifty-eight feet and six inches (or eighteen metres) battering to this top expanse of forty-five feet and six inches (or fourteen metres). We looked down to ground level over a really solid parapet wall, four feet high, some forty-two feet (or thirteen metres) below.

I had a feeling of pride in those workmen for achieving this enormous edifice. Very few people walking round and admiring this pagoda, unless they have a picture in their mind of the struggle of how to build the place, will understand how this all came about. It would take several pages to do this building justice, but, briefly, it has three roof levels, each one being set back a little, all with flowing hips with dragons guarding. The main structure is a good solid brick building, with stone columns taking the roof's overhang, the corner ones all slightly on the batter (or leaning inwards).

It must have been a very intimidating sight for would-be invaders of this ancient city to have seen, all those centuries ago.

A visit then to south of the city to see the Big Goose Pagoda. Lee told us a story of how it got its name. A flock of geese flew over a monastery, when one fell out of the heavens, quite dead, to the ground. The monks decided it was a saint and built a pagoda to its body. There is also a smaller Little Goose Pagoda, which resembles the larger one, but was built at a much later date, only a few kilometres away. As we kept criss-crossing the Wall encircling the city and each time seeing at first hand the magnitude of it, I asked Lee whether she had any idea how many workmen originally were employed. A quick answer: "About 300,000 men working both winter and summer.

4th March: first we take a visit to a factory which makes quarter-scale identikits of the Terracotta Army we were to see later. We saw the first piece of clay shaped, the various pieces, legs, arms, heads, et cetera, all fired in a kiln, and then—what a masterpiece!—the end product. *And this* was not the Real Thing! So what was the size of the army guarding the Emperor? Then another Friendship Shop, and more money changing hands.

On the way to the Chambers of the Terracotta Warriors, Lee pointed out to us more Tombs of Emperors, their wives, high officials, and their wives. She made it quite clear to us that if exploration work was to be carried out around this area of several square miles in future years, seven villages and seven factories would have to be destroyed and demolished. Arriving at last at our destination, we discovered a huge dome of plastic sheeting on lightweight steel framing that covered the whole area of 12,000 square metres. No cameras were allowed, and there were guards on duty at various places as you walked round. A boarded enclosure with a sensible five-foot-high guard rail gave us all adequate protection along and around the perimeter. We followed Lee anti-clockwise. There they all were—the Terracotta Warriors, eleven parallel pits, running east to west all drawn up in battle formation, with three rows each of seven archers being used as the vanguards. There was a single column of spearmen facing and looking outwards to us, and a central group of thirty-eight lines of infantry and chariots.

WHAT A SIGHT!

Most of the wood that the chariots were made of has disappeared, but the terracotta horses with their fittings that pulled them together are there for us all to witness and marvel at. The army as you could see, were provided with no makeshift rubbish; they were equipped with equipment of excellent quality, bronze arms consisting of swords, daggers, short spears, halberds, axes, crossbows all of wood (though sadly now almost gone through time, but the fittings are there as well as the arrowheads). Lee tells us that lots of different elements were used, as many as ten were applied to some of the armoury. Each weapon when they were discovered was still sharp and untarnished though under, in some parts, tons of clay and soil.

The figures we were looking at all were about five feet six inches tall (or one metre seven centimetres).

No doubt when made they were all larger than life, then firing in their preparation would have brought them to this size. The upper part of the body is solid clay, the lower part and legs hollowed. It appears the bodies could have been mass-produced, but something struck me—you could not mass produce the facial expressions. Each one as you passed by had, to put it bluntly, a different face—happy, contented, laughing, beaming, thoughtful, sad, considerate. You could even spot the conscientious ones. I was lost for words. We had seen the model factory earlier in the day, but this was the real thing. The hands, legs and heads, as Lee told us, were luted together with the bodies, enabling a variety of positions, especially of hands, which, as you could see, were holding reins, swords, spears and other weapons in different grasps. Also the face modelling which seemed uncannily to fit the figure, was extraordinary. Had we noticed? "Yes, we have," we replied in unison.

It was some time before I latched onto the blob on top of some of the figures' heads. Lee explained that they all have long hair; the hair is dressed and shaped round in all sorts of fashion, single buns, but chiefly double buns. It appears this sort of hairstyle was very masculine, right from the Emperor Qin dynasty to the mid-seventeenth century. The guards on the outside of the formation wore armour, possibly of lacquered leather in small squares, while those on the inside appeared to be unprotected. The figures, Lee pointed out, were all painted originally. What a sight that must have been, and, sure thing, if you looked closely, you could see faint traces of the paint. Each of the chambers was covered in timber and you could see where part of the wood is charred owing to an attempt to plunder the chambers by a later emperor. Continuing on round, the next chamber excavated was L-shaped; it contained about 1,000 figures including four chariots, cavalry leading horses, foot soldiers, crossbow men. One tall majestic soldier stood out a mile, standing some 1.9 metres. Lee said he was a general. Another chamber, where work was in progress, contained one chariot with some seventy soldiers. There was a lot of excavation still to be done here. Several Chinese archaeologists were very carefully doing what archaeologists do. I asked Lee how they found this treasure. In 1974, she said two farmers were digging for a new well and, when five metres down, they came across a couple of terracotta warriors' heads, then bodies. Digging deeper, legs and boots were uncovered, the authorities told. Since then, this wonderful find has gone from strength to strength. It was only then that I realised that what we were now looking at had been covered with fifteen foot of earth. It explained why all the soldiers were in parallel lines–imagine how a tunnel is made by first sinking a shaft and then removing earth from the tunnel like a mine. As you move further into the ground, there will be timber supports all round to protect diggers and what is held dear for future reference. In this case, no doubt, there was just a gradient running down to the entrances and remember there are eleven of those. The mind boggles! I wonder how they saw or what light was available to place these so accurately, as I was now gazing down on them just a few feet away.

When the Emperor Qin ascended the throne, he was only thirteen years of age, and, right from the start, he was building all this, plus his own tumulus some one and a half miles away. Lee told us that he was surrounded by warriors throughout his lifetime, and always wanted this protection for his afterlife. There must have been good and bad faults in Emperor Qin, reign 221-209BC. He was most famous, or rather notorious, as a bad person for his burning of books. Any book that would give knowledge to his people was removed, taken and destroyed by fire. Only farming books survived, since such knowledge would not endanger the Emperor's intellectual stronghold. The authors had to go too—no, they were not burnt but buried alive. His good points: he must have had a wonderful employment scheme going all over the country after he had united the whole of China—the Great Wall, temples, palaces, as well as roads that were built to take nine vehicles wide. When you think that the old horse and cart was six feet wide, originally a road must have looked like a motorway without the central reservation. A workforce of 700,000 men and women were employed on his own tumulus. For how long? I would suggest several decades.

In the museum nearby, were another two pieces of magical wonder—two bronze chariots, one in especially good condition. Both are a quarter life-size, but what workmanship! Both have been restored as they were originally and all the parts are movable. No, you can't touch them. There are four horses to draw each chariot. Windows in the covered chariot open and close to let the passengers inside have fresh air if required, the horses' harnesses are inlaid with gold and silver and all decorated over their foreheads with colourful plumes. It appears that a replica of one of the chariots was presented to our Queen Elizabeth II on her visit to Xian in the autumn of 1987.

Outside now, we were able to take photos again. My company and I agreed we had just seen another wonder of the world. Truly wonderful! On our way back for lunch, we passed the emperor's tumulus. When Lee told us what it was, there were gasps of astonishment. Rising two hundred and sixty feet and stretching five hundred yards in diameter, even from quite a distance away, it looked very imposing. She told us no person has ever seen inside, and there is only supposition as to what it contains; perhaps other tour parties received a different explanation. "For there is heaven when you look up at the ceiling, *no-one on the earth was more important to the emperor than heaven.*" She also told us that all those workers were ultimately put to death as then no one knew for what purpose the tumults were and where the locality might be. She then told us it might also be a hoax, as he might not be buried there at all.

In the afternoon our first visit was to a kindergarten very similar to the one at Chendge, but there were no boarding pupils here. The children all seemed, again, very keen on showing us their handiwork. We then visited, by kind permission of the owners, a few houses nearby. We were all invited in and made welcome. Just the scantiest of furniture, family heirlooms, portraits of families long since departed and the barest of covering over the stone floors. It looked like a kind of lino. I had a quick look in the bathroom; the old-fashioned cast-iron bath was half-filled with water. I presumed someone was going to take a dip shortly, but no, there was a fish swimming about, quite happy and contented—perhaps some fifteen inches long, I enquired of Lee for what purpose this was (asking this only to have my thoughts confirmed). She replied, "It is a trout and it is the family's evening meal, caught this morning, this very good food for healthy body." So not singing for their supper, but swimming for their supper!

We were soon on the way to the next Friendship store, with, as usual, plenty of hold-ups. The windows of our coach were open and a familiar noise came in—phut, phut, phut, phut. And there it was. Fred and Margaret, a couple from Leicester had seen it too, and of course we had seen hundreds and hundreds of them. It was a steam-driven tractor, less than five feet in length and three feet high, fired by coal and deep orange in colour. With just a faint wisp of smoke from its exhaust pipe, it was pulling a large load of vegetables. Seeing this, I considered the situation in China as wherever we had travelled, small businesses trading coal heaps were always close to the highways, so feeding the gluttonous tractors, replenishing their furnaces. One wondered what were they doing to the atmosphere. In our little country back home, pollution of the environment is now at the front of everybody's minds. I did mention this later to Lee, who assured me this was all under control with forms of filters to help purify the air.

An early start next morning, as we had to pick up the flight back to Beijing at eleven-thirty. Lee again found us some remarkable places to visit, first Da Ming village. Here a procession met us, highly decorative, four attendants plus a chariot. Lee told us this was part of a regular performance for tourists, and anyone was welcome to ride and be carried by the now buoyantly cheerful company. Most of us were now low on our own budgets of yuan allocated to our trip to Xian, but the spectacle gave you a good insight into a carried carriage being conveyed for the Emperor, his wives and entourage, and the number of carriages needed for those dynasties long-departed.

Next we made a stop at my request, as I had for a long time wondered what those poly-covered buildings contained, quite often in open fields. Just John and I got out, both armed with our cameras. The building in question had a long red brick wall, forty feet long, twelve feet high and about eighteen feet wide, with a dwarf red-brick wall eighteen inches high forming a sizeable lean-to glass house. But no glass—instead, a bamboo-framed structure that was being uncovered by a Chinese couple who were rolling up a concertina-type of straw roller, attached by bamboo to the high part of the wall which left the polythene sheeting covering the delicates inside. But what delicates! Finding a small aperture in the vertical walling and looking inside, lo and behold, there were tomato plants with three trusses showing, the first one almost set. Back in the bus, Lee told us that up to three crops are grown during the year, also pumpkins, courgettes, cucumbers, peppers and lettuce. Inside in the summer it is almost unbearable to work, as the tomatoes are green one day and red the next. Just a wry smile with the last remark.

Our final visit was to look at part of the Tang Dynasties city limits, which was bigger than all the others. Not a lot remains here, but Lee informed us that it was a very long wall which encircled the city, perhaps three times as long as the existing one. She said this was in urgent need of finances to rebuild the parts that were going into decay. Somebody said, "It's the same tune in our country." She laughed with us saying, "Yes, I understand."

On our flight back to Beijing, the Chinese air stewardess made us feel like Emperor Qin's family. Everyone remarked that the kindness and consideration were something special. Peter was at the airport to meet us, saying we were to have lunch straightaway, as soon as we have unpacked, so a quick wash and brush up. More and more of us were using chopsticks, which if handled right, and if the pieces selected to sustain oneself were of the right size, were passable.

At two p.m. Peter arrived with Mr Shrew, for our destination was to be Beijing's Temple of Heaven. Again, this is an outstanding piece of planning, where the temples and halls are carefully plotted to cause the authentic environment very little inconvenience. It is set in the centre of a park of six hundred and sixty-six acres. Peter told us it was destroyed by fire several times and was last rebuilt in 1890. The next temple we saw, in fact, was a hall, The Hall of Prayer for Good Harvests. Now this is one hundred and twenty-eight feet high, perfectly round and constructed without the use of any nails. I cannot recall seeing any larger dowels, mortises and tenons than what I was seeing now. The roof was made up of three levels, gradually reducing in size. As to the blue roof tiles, I would not even like to guess how much they weighed each, or the total covering for that matter. The blue was now faded, but when completed over a hundred years ago it was a pale shade of blue, symbolising the colour of heaven. What a striking building it still is with a gold ball on the summit. Peter reminded us that all the buildings were used for what their appropriate names signified. The Palace of Abstinence—I could not see myself how this could be of any benefit to anybody, but the emperor at the time had this built for exactly that purpose, to abstain. He would spend a night fasting and be celibate, before carrying out his duties next morning. This would occur the exact middle of each month. He begged the spirits and gods of the sun and moon, clouds and rain, thunder and lightning to not only bless himself and his family, but all his subjects, and he prayed for the coming harvests to be of the highest quality, and in abundance.

You can see how important each and every temple, hall or building was in playing its part in the making of Chinese culture.

When we saw a circular marble terrace, I thought we had seen it all. Then Peter told us that the next day we were going to see, walk round and admire a marble boat.

That night our evening meal was taken on the thirty-second floor of one of the highest hotel diners at the time in Beijing. The lifts took you up and down in seconds. Only six of us were to sample the Peking Duck, as we were all asked to view the poor thing before the action. On arrival some twenty minutes later, the meal had been shredded into pieces suitable for chopstick operations—as the waiter informed us, manageable portions. Dish after dish of succulent oriental foods were placed in front of us, but most of us were now suffering from the dreaded lurgy—Asian Flu.

Early start yet again, as we have to pack and be clear of our rooms by ten a.m. The suitcases were left with the concierge, as on the dot of nine a.m. our new guide Denis, who was to look after us this morning, arrived.

My cold was little improved—Sandra and Terry? The latter had a shocker starting, Mary the travel agent had one, also most of the other nine people. All looked queasy except for Jean, who yesterday outshone us all, together with John and Pat, by climbing up a daunting pagoda some two hundred and twenty feet high. I would have loved to have accomplished this, and if there had been a lift down, I would certainly have tried.

Our first stop was the zoo. We only had about an hour to look and walk round, so we hardly had time to take photos. When we arrived at the panda area, all seven seemed quite happy and contented chewing on their bamboo shoots. It was quite an open zoo, where the animals had nice areas for themselves and they obviously did not appear to be suffering from the prevailing conditions, not like their human counterparts with their overcoats, scarves, gloves, and noses as red as any Xmas reindeer.

Moving on, it came on us all of a sudden–the Emperor's Summer Palace, yes, another one here in Beijing. It made me wonder how many Summer Palaces there were in China. But the one I had seen in Chendge and the one we were about to see were quite different. The first thing as you walked in that you could not avoid noticing was the long corridor. Looking through, it seemed to run for miles, but as we walked along admiring the spellbinding pieces of artistry, you had the feeling this indeed was special. It ran parallel to the lake on the north shore, so linking all the buildings into one huge area. Just along this half-mile walkway there are over 14,000 paintings, all taken from Chinese mythology and literature, all species of birds, all flowers wild or cultivated, trees, boats, ships, bridges, small delicate paintings, big bold ones, amongst many hundreds of everyday objects you would observe. The whole corridor was open to the lake on one side and the temples bordered the lake on the other side. The roof above us was supported by eight-inch square timbers standing some

eight feet high. Four pavilions break up this enchantment;
each one of these has eight-inch round timbers, same
height of eight feet, more like pill boxes. Each one has a
name, Retain the Good, Living with the Ripples, Autumn
Water and Clear and Far Pavilion.

The paintings are all joined up for the whole length,
the rafters, binders, purlins, lintels, plates, columns,
nothing is missed. I can assure you my neck ached like the
dickens as I with my companions were almost struck dumb
at this marathon work. Denis our guide told us, "This is
like your Forth Bridge; as soon as cleaners and repairers
reach the end, they go back and start again." I asked him
if the wood lintels we passed under were painted on the
top, the fourth side that we could not see. He looked at me
with disbelief, as if I dared doubt those workmen of 1750.
"Of course it's painted on the top," he replied.

The architects who designed this must have realised this
was indeed something special, not only for the millions of
people who have wandered through, soaking up this
extraordinary marvel, but for the hundreds of locals who
come here at dawn's early light to do their constitutionals.
I am sure Jean would have been one of the first down
here, as she had already indulged in keep-fit exercises in
one of the parks near our hotel. Denis kept calling out to
come along, as we must hurry. For myself, I could have
taken a deckchair and gradually dissected each bay
thoroughly before leaving, for, as I had never or perhaps
would never again see the like, I was totally fascinated. At
the end of the walk, was the marble boat. You have to
cross the emperor's gateway to step aboard. It is truly
marble but not very thick. The original one was built in
1755 but was destroyed by fire in 1860, and then rebuilt

in 1893. The Empress CIXI wanted something different, and as there was an American influence around at the time, she had marble waterwheels added so it looked like a Mississippi Paddle Steamer. It certainly looks the part.

Mirrors have been positioned on both the lower and upper decks, which then reflect the scenes on the lake, to increase her pleasure when she took tea here on nice afternoons. The boat itself is again a work of art, and craftsmanship. As I walked around, it made you wonder how the roof kept up, supported on slender round marble columns; the two on the forward part of the boat were much stouter in diameter than the others on the upper deck. Evidently, it had a timber-framed structure, so the marble adornments are not so heavily committed, thus not so fragile as a first appearance belies. No doubt, checks are made periodically on the timbers, which I must say were quite difficult to see. Part of a marble seat had wood showing through, but this was the only piece I observed. How much the roof weighed, I did not manage to find out, but knowing the class and quality of other previous buildings of that era and earlier, this was not "a throw-me-up-quick job". Everywhere you looked, I am confident it was as it was all those years ago, in pristine condition and pleasing to the eye.

Back into the long walk, Denis told us that Chinese couples meet here for the first time, the friendship moves rapidly on, and by the end of walk, (remember nearly half a mile of walking through a picture gallery) marriage has been discussed and in most cases agreed between the couples. Passing through a large decorative opening, Pai Yun Diaw (Hall that Dispels the Clouds) was directly in front of us. Further up Longevity Hill, rising from a wall-like foundation, is the one hundred-and-fifty-foot high Fo Xian Ge, (Fragrance of Buddha) Pagoda, and on the very top of the hill Zhi Hui Hai, (Sea of Wisdom Temple). Both the latter ones were built by Buddhas. I can imagine what it must be like for tour managers in the summer months, and passed those thoughts on to Denis, who said it was bedlam.

Lunch back in our hotel with the afternoon at leisure. I decided that as I had still not seen Tianamein Square, I would take a taxi and pay a visit. Eight Yuan, just about one pound, was the fare. The driver dropped me off in a side street; you cannot stop anywhere around the Square as it's one-way, traffic only stopping at crossings and then not to let people alight or climb aboard. A zebra crossing gave me access to the Square. I suppose I was about two-thirds of the way down and on my immediate right was the one hundred-and-twenty-foot high monument to The People's Hero, made of granite in 1958. I caught myself holding my breath again at the enormity of the Square. I likened the whole area to one I had been associated with many moons ago–playing football on Hackney Marches (when you looked on the notice board to find you were playing on pitch no 22, you could see those goalposts a distance away). But this was all concrete, no grass, only a few brave weeds poking through the joints. The whole expanse is bewildering; the biting winds moving across made this feel like the Arctic Circle. The statue seems very appropriately situated, as several bloody demonstrations have taken place here, the last one as we know in 1989. An enclosure with an army guard standing on a small podium seemed to be a big attraction to the photographers who were out in their hundreds. Walking back down the

Square to the mausoleum built in ten months by 70,000 volunteers, you can quite understand how buildings take shape overnight, as the labour force is so intense, it makes you wonder how they are so accurately constructed.

What a sight the interior is—Chairman Mao's resting place, huge tapestries of countryside scenes, hills, rivers, birds, wild flowers, all of which Chairman Mao would have been associated with during his lifetime. As you walk round in single file on the highly polished marble floors, you see a crystal coffin containing his embalmed body. To perceive the contentment on his features is surely a miracle in itself. I suppose the surroundings have a lot to do with this, satisfaction, serenity, peacefulness, it's all around you in volumes as you file past a few feet from the man the country held in such high esteem.

Outside, more last-minute purchases from about a couple of dozen canvas-covered gift and souvenir stalls. My last cuppa of Rosy Lee, which I enjoyed immensely and which did a lot to improve my feelings even though I had three pullovers and a cardigan on. I made my way to what I thought was a taxi terminus, (the place where I had been dropped off). No! Wrong street, nothing unusual, my own navigation, but I quickly made progress, arriving to find a Chinese couple who were going to the same hotel, so we shared the expense.

A quick wash and I changed into travelling clothes and footwear. There were a lot of goodbyes, one especially from myself to Billy the porter, who had been so helpful to me when I was almost down and out. At the airport a big thank you and a firm handshake from Peter, I for one had appreciated how much he had tried to sell his country's development and culture. Flight No CA955's boarding soon came over the Tannoy, nine-fifty p.m. on the dot, takes off upwards and homewards. Now looking round the aircraft you realised, by their paper tissues, just how many passengers were affected by the lurgy. I would say at a guess a third were performing this nasal duty.

Settling back in my seat, taking a last quick look as the lights of Beijing faded from my view, I realised that indeed this was the return flight, and all those occurrences that I witnessed those past ten days were real and not fictitious. I seemed to have a feeling of satisfaction. I had made contact with just a fraction of its 1.2 billion people, knew a little of them and could identify with their everyday life. Settling back still further in my not-too-comfortable seat, I recapped on a few of the experiences that I had been part of. The entry system, it's certainly a lot of red tape, but it works. The various methods of transportation, they all work, perhaps there should be a special mention for the bus service. This was my first experience of seeing an overcrowded bus, of course I had seen photos and documentaries from various countries, but I had not observed anything like this first-hand. I saw a bus and seemed mesmerised by it, hundreds upon hundreds of times, I watched it, wondered, stunned how the springs seemed permanently the opposite way to how they are made to sustain loads. The passengers must have offered a prayer before boarding for their safe journey to their destination, but I can truthfully say that I did not see one at any time broken down.

Health care, provisions for young and old, simple, uncomplicated, they work. Food and drink, both no doubt once you were used to them, gave you fulfilment. Whenever looking at local residents of the place visited, you saw rice, vegetables chopped quite small, dumplings, chicken, duck, mutton and beef. Local beers, all enjoyable and appetising, the wine, drinkable–they all looked healthy and contented with what was their sustainment. The employment system: it seems half the population work, the other half keep the country clean and wholesome, nobody's idle and that's for sure. The building trade with new hotels planned or partially completed seems to have got its act together, and first-class hotels are our, the tourists' benefits. They are going up, especially in Beijing, at the rate of knots. Whenever I had the opportunity my attention was always taken aback by their methods of accomplishing their trade. Be it carpenter, painter, bricklayer or whoever, all seemed to have a short length of workspace to perform their own discipline, I have seen as many as ten bricklayers, and the same amount of minders working on a wall twenty-five feet in length. As you can gather, this is unusual by comparison with our methods, but it works. To see a new building with miles of bamboo scaffolding round the total area is something that is not easily forgotten. It does not look safe, and no building inspector would even think of passing it as fit to work on in the Western world.

The Chinese tradesmen are not only happy with this situation but first-class results are achieved.

The Chinese who I had dealings with, staff, workers, guides, shopkeepers, army, police, in fact all walks of life seemed to be of the same nature–conscientious, cheerful, and caring. One of many highlights that I enjoyed seeing immensely, and is still puzzling me to this day is, no, not the Great Wall of China, nor the Terracotta Warriors, but the thirty-two columns of Mawmu wood at The Hall of

Sacrifice in the Ming Tomes. Whew! I can see them now and how satiny to touch. As I described earlier, I cannot recall seeing wood of that age looking so beautiful. Perhaps a more appropriate name than the one used might be Radiant Perfection. What is astonishing is that they came from South West China, hundreds of miles away, maybe 1,500 miles. They could never have been transported by road, as those trees were perhaps up to 100 feet in length. Why this length you might ask?! The person in charge of timbers of this description, knew and could decide for himself, the uses that it could be put to, beams, purlins, rafters. Each part could be sawn for its structural duties, and then every single piece had to play its part in that wonderful building.

My own theory is they came the same way as the stone came for the Pyramids of Egypt—by water. Most likely, other large timber structures around China came the same way, I never dreamed at the time to ask any of our tour managers about this, one of them would be bound to have known.

It seems to me that only a small minority of Chinese realise how fortunate they are to have such a wealth of hidden history bursting at the seams to be let loose. I trust this, though not in my lifetime, will be nurtured and cared for by generations to come, and accomplished within qualified channels.

Gatwick eight a.m. (GMT) Sunday, 7th March. After a long plod with our luggage, nursing a red nose, and finally going through Customs, I thanked my companions especially those in my company on our trip to Chendge. I cannot speak too highly of them, as they made that visit so gratifying, and had me to thank for my cold starting a mini epidemic.

At the development stage of my photos, I was very pleased with my camera; the success rate was better than I had expected. None of the photos came out over the Himalayas; the rail ones I think were average.

We all had the chance when we were at Chendge to have purchased a tape of ourselves, yes all five of us had been seen on National Television. We all saw it, it would have cost £20.00. My life, much wiser after the event! Yes I should like to visit China again, perhaps in late spring or early summer, when perhaps a visit would be more appropriate.

A Canadian Experience

I was one of the last of our party to arrive for our holiday in the Canadian Rockies, only to be told by our tour manager Roseanne that our flight had been delayed by one hour, so it would now be midday instead of eleven a.m., our scheduled flight time this day 30th September 1993. The delay allowed me some two hours to browse through the duty-free shops to purchase films, and, for my microcassette recorder, a few tapes.

I had been delayed, since I started out at seven-thirty a.m. on my journey across London, with both underground and mainline connections. Even as early as this the plot was taking shape, indicating that clocks and time-keeping were going to play an important role whilst I was on my first visit to Canada. Delays disrupt even the best-organised administration. At noon we were up and away. The lady passenger in the other aisle seat opposite was soon pleasantly engaged in a conversation with me—a very charming tour manager she turned out to be, going to the same destination, Calgary, and meeting a tour group, which appeared, from the various places that she mentioned on her programme, to be almost identical to my own one.

During the flight, I had probably the most rewarding and satisfying ten minutes of my whole life, through my asking a stewardess, if I could pay a visit to the pilot.

"Yes, certainly come up straightaway."

And, certain I wasn't going to miss this treat, I was soon up with the captain on his flight deck. Both his co-pilots were mines of information, describing in detail each of several banks of dials and clocks, each containing indicators, some large, others very small. Some were even over our heads. They soon explained how every single one plays a major part in keeping this aircraft in the air, and, of course, in our safety.

I remarked on the smallness of the cabin, as it seemed rather a cramped situation for an aeroplane of such importance, I was immediately told by the captain, "The benefit of being on the small side is because its large percentage is visibility."

And looking outside, you had to agree.

On being told that we were flying at 33,100 feet, and that we were just passing over the tip of Greenland, I said, "I did not realise that we were so far off course."

"No, we aren't," the captain replied. "In fact we are exactly to our flight path, but the reason is that, as you know, the earth is round and it's shorter not to fly in a straight line." Then turning and checking with both dials and his wristwatch, he nodded and added, "Dead on our scheduled time of arrival."

I don't mind telling you that the windows here were huge compared to the passenger seat windows (and there you were lucky to find one not scratched).

The scene below, no doubt an everyday vista to my hosts, (if they chose to look) weather permitting, was stunning. It was apparent that the magnificent portrait that lay beneath us bewildered me.

The captain said, "You look as if you have seen a ghost."

I just mumbled something, as it was so difficult to find words that expressed the beauty that lay below me. I followed this sight until I had moved to the very last area of glass in the cabin, then turned to the captain and said, "I don't suppose I shall ever see anything like that again." For what I had seen, as far as the eye could see, was the snow-covered coastline of cliffs, looking like teeth from prehistoric monsters, the jaws biting into the emerald green of the Atlantic Ocean, and no doubt an overture being played by the hundreds upon hundreds of seagulls wheeling in aerial acrobatics. And even at this great height I could so vividly observe them far below. "Just magic." Thanking them and shaking their hands, they bade me a pleasant journey and a safe one.

On arrival at Calgary and having gone quickly through customs, we collected our luggage and those who owned them altered their time-pieces by putting them back seven hours. Now dusk had fallen, and outside the airport terminal we all had our first introductions to Henry, who was to be, for the next six days, not only our driver but also baggage-master as well—the end of a long tiring, bewildering and yet a great day.

Day 2 dawned with a clear blue sky that promised much. Henry, who we all had met for such a short time was quickly on Christian-name terms with us all. Our baggage carefully stored away, our surprise was that this was the first time that Roseanne, the tour leader and he had met, for even at this early stage, they had an enormous shared knowledge of Canada, its people and culture. First on our day's programme was a visit to the Calgary Fort, founded in 1875 as a Northwest Mounted Police base. Its museum is filled with period pieces from Red Indians and Mounted Police memorabilia, carefully preserved in this log building.

Next a visit to the site of the winter Olympics of 1988: the buildings are astonishing, and there is even a facsimile of the Crest Toboggan run, upon which Jean, whose company I was in, and I sat together for half-price, as we are both OAPs. You look at a giant screen and as you watch the twists and turns appear in front of you, so you are tipped up and down, and from side to side. What a great thrill it must be for real! We emerged none the worse for our experience, having thoroughly enjoyed it Then it was on to the University of Calgary, which appears to be home to almost every nation of students upon earth. The entrance has a modern sculpture of stainless steel tubes, of massive diameter and length, and inside there is an ice rink with a central island. We all thought it rather unique, as the entrance to the ice rink is via a tunnel directly under the ice leading to the changing areas! The whole structure is covered by an unusually shaped roof, which appears to have very little support. I would like to have investigated this further, but as Henry kept reminding us:

"We have a long day ahead of us."

So my thoughts on its construction had to be stored away for the time being.

Next stop? A race track where the "Stampede City!"

events are staged. During the short break for photos, I noticed how many of us were snappers—ninety per cent it seemed. In our foreground were the horses being trained, beyond this the "Saddledome", a striking building with the roof constructed exactly like a huge saddle, and, far in the distance, the snow-capped peaks of the Canadian Rockies. Even at this distance, they seemed an awesome sight, a fact remarked by every one of the twenty-eight people who made up our tour group, busy snapping away from this fairly high position 3,500 feet above Calgary.

Back in the coach, and onward to Banff.

"Banff is indeed the heart of the Rockies." Henry, very seldom lost for words, enthused over the various mountain rivers that passed us by. As we dropped down to Banff, the buffalo-shaped mountain covered with pine forest looked from a distance just like a charging one, very lifelike.

Our hotel was the Rimrock, only opened the year before our visit and Japanese-owned. It is built on the side of a mountain, with most of the floor below road level; my room was on the seventh floor, just one floor up from the entrance. My first impression was of a small building, but I was never more wrong: the architect had carved out huge chunks of mountainside to give a first-time visitor the appearance of it being tight for space. The hotel was thus as near as possible to the highway, only about forty feet away (all under cover) so that you could step out from the coach to face the excellent welcome bestowed upon us.

Our rooms were at the rear of the hotel overlooking the views across the valley; this included the famous Banff Spring Hotel. The pine, spruce and larch trees were interspersed spasmodically with groups of aspen trees in their autumnal colours of varied reds and gold. What a spectacular sight this was, and one that had quite a few people visiting my balcony at sunrise and sunset for photographs. Fortunately the weather was always kind to us.

My room (entrance was made by employing a card about the size of a playing one, which had to be inserted correctly for the door to open), had to be the size of a dining room with two king-size beds, two huge wardrobes, floor-to-ceiling, three tables, a suite of furniture, and a television set which gave me, if I wanted, a choice of fifty channels. Judging by its size, it must have arrived in the room in the first instance with some difficulty. During my stay, I once pressed the wrong button on the remote control to find not only my name and address, but also my passport number displayed on the screen.

Day 3! The coach arrived at about nine a.m., our first stop being the Hot Springs. In fact directly opposite our hotel, an overflow stream was flowing quite happily in a channel beside the main road.

The Banff Hot Springs were discovered in 1883 by brothers William and Tom McCardell, and their partner Frank McCabe. Their first sighting stimulated plans for them becoming rich by building a bathing/health resort. If only they could become owners of the springs and surrounding land! However, they were not the first ones to have discovered the cave and hot springs. But certainly they can lay claim to bringing the area to public attention. They also unwittingly helped to bring about the setting up of the National Park. Arguments followed over the legal rights and ownership of the area in question. The government of the time was called into resolve it. This was done by proclaiming it would belong to all Canadians as part of Canada's first National Park, now also a Heritage Park.

On going to the caves and hot springs, it was apparent that very few alterations have been made since they were first discovered—only the introduction, regulated by law of walkways, of guard-rails and lighting that has been beneficial to all nationalities alike. Reading and digesting how the springs tick over, I learnt that the waters you see are made up of the snow and rain that fall on the mountain above us, ending in the mighty Bow River below us. But some of the water filters through cracks and pores in the rock, to a depth of some two miles below the surface of the mountain. On its descent, it becomes hotter and hotter, heated by the radioactive decay in the earth. It is like a coffee percolator! When boiling it is under great pressure, and must seek a cooler atmosphere higher up. Depending upon its speed to the surface, and (most important) the degree to which it mixes with the cold ground water, this is then routed very hot to the hot springs, or just above tepid to the Cave and Basin end. The smell was at times very unpleasant, but, myself used to country smells, I found it bearable.

"Well! Why does it smell?"

When the water becomes heated it is able to dissolve minerals from the rock—pyrite (copper and iron) and gypsum (lime) are the two common sulphur-bearing minerals being dissolved in the springs, giving off the smell of rotten eggs. This is produced when the dissolving minerals are broken down by sulphate oxidising bacteria in the water! Before that is, it comes to the surface.

Quite a few of our party are already leaving as it is getting too much for them. I have taken several snaps, but I doubt if my camera flash and speed is equal to the vapours rising from the water, nor to the lighting and surroundings. However, a number of experts from the photography world are with us with their zoom lenses, et cetera, and talking to them, they assure me that it's worth trying. As one said, "You may not came this way again."

All the water has to finish up somewhere and as I mentioned earlier, some of it flows down the hill opposite the hotel; other streams are also going towards the Cave and Basin end; here there is marshland that we saw only briefly. Henry tells us the warm rich waters have formed a rich oasis for many different plant and bird life.

Multitudes of small fish and insects provide food in abundance for all the needy–a Canadian Rockies' paradise giving pleasure to all who can visit and take advantage of this environment.

Next: a visit to the Banff Spring Hotel, an unforgettable experience! What an attraction this is summer and winter. Its Victorian standards are wherever you care to place a foot. This I do not doubt at all is why the patrons keep coming back year after year, regardless of the advancement of customer improvements elsewhere.

Back on board, we take a quick trip to see the Bow River Falls. This is where the mighty Bow River and Spey River meet. Looking at this great piece of natural water and chatting to Rosanne, I said, "I would like to have a go at some white-water rafting, if it was possible while I'm here."

"No, not around here, but more probable at Jasper, where the water levels are more benign and ensure safer rafting."

The tunnel-mountain drive gave Henry another opportunity to tell us more about the mountains, their peculiarities, their names and how they got them. There followed a drive back to Banff and a trip up the sulphur mountain by gondola. Part of the internals we had seen earlier; each of the gondolas held four people and again comfort was provided with excellent seating. On the mountaintop the Rockies appeared as an endless forbidding horizon, with snow-capped peaks seemingly surrounding us. I knew the temperature around us was pretty cold, and remarked, like quite a few others, "I would not like to be there in the winter." Somebody mentioned that it would be in the region of thirty below, I shivered at the thought.

What did stand out, even at this height, was the Buffalo- (or Bison-) shaped mountain, which I mentioned earlier. The whole shape was covered in a blanket of fir forest, maybe hundreds of yards long and very high. I thought a bit special.

Day 4. This day was for us to do as we pleased. A number of us decided to take a trip on Lake Millewanka, and, as the weather promised to be in our favour, we were quickly organised. Two taxis took us to the lake, about a half an hour away, so the ten of us found this a reasonable package. Then a small boat conveyed us on a very tranquil excursion—the scenery, the solitude, and the chatter of our captain. She was quite young; I don't think I would be exaggerating if I said fifteen, and certainly she knew her stuff, giving her passengers confidence in her capabilities. On the return leg down the other side of the lake, she asked if anyone wanted to take the wheel. John, who has a boat on the Thames, quickly took up this offer; his wife Margaret declined, but their friend Sheila took over for a spell. I turned the offer down; I knew there was no traffic, but things "could" happen...I thought, looking at the rocky foreshore. Back to the hotel, and time to write a few postcards, which was to take me some two hours, for darkness had fallen by the time I had completed them. I had a quick wash and brush up, and went out to the bus stop that was right outside the entrance. There was a courtesy bus laid on by the management, running at half-hourly intervals for the ten-minute run into Banff. This was to be highly recommended as it allowed us to be more economical with our expenditure, given that the hotel meals and bar prices were not agreeable to some of our pockets.

Day 5! I was the last to board the coach, and I had promised Henry I would help with the baggage. Oh, the comfort of that bed! Rosanne, wagging a finger at me, said, "You know, Percy, we have a long day ahead of us." On the coach, Henry is again in top form. Quite often, you get coach drivers who are a mine of information, with voices that do nothing but demand attention. Henry was one of them; as everybody agrees his pleasant Canadian drawl seems even more dramatic as he reaches the punch-lines of his stories.

The highway we are travelling on is a direct route to Jasper, and was completed in 1940. In 1990, its fiftieth anniversary was celebrated and a large number of the original workforce was invited to share the big day with the staff at that time.

No vehicles over 4,500 kilograms are allowed on the

highway, and speed restrictions are rigorously enforced, with "on-the-spot fines".

In fact, this is one of the busiest highways in the Rockies, and after a lot of pressure on the government by hauliers of all denominations, they have agreed legislation for a four-lane highway through the National Park. There has been opposition to this, especially around Jasper, where people do not want to see change; some people there would sooner revert back to a single passage in and out of Jasper. As Henry reminds us, "You can't stop progress." Following the sign-posting to Lake Louise, Henry tells us it was not discovered until 1888. Until then the whole area was "taboo" for all the native Red Indians. It was always held with great respect, as the noises that echoed along the valley were like "thunder", appearing to them as a sign of the gods' displeasure.

Tom Wilson, a surveyor, working for his company Canadian Pacific Railway, had been detailed by his boss, Major Rogers, to survey this particular area for extensions to the rail network. One day he had made camp in a valley, when he heard what he thought was a clap of thunder and looking to the sky noticed it was cloudless. So what was making the noise? After some thought, he decided to break camp and investigate. The Red Indian scouts would have none of this—it did not matter how much persuading or what rewards were offered for that matter, they would take no part. So leaving his second-in-command in charge, Tom and a few companions left with supplies and equipment. The Red Indians were convinced they would not return.

As they headed further upwards, the noises—rumbling and crashing sounds—got closer, and at times they could hardly hear each other talking. When they arrived they found that the deafening "thunder claps" were pieces of glacier breaking off (called cavins) and crashing into the lake. Henry says, "It must have been that terrible sound which had struck terror and fear into the Red Indians, probably for thousands of years." Originally the lake was called "the Lake of Little Fishes", named after the third daughter of Queen Victoria, Princess Louise Caroline Alberta, who married the Duke of Borne in 1871. In 1878 he came out to be the Governor General of Canada, and they both stayed for eight years. He was later to become the ninth Duke of Argyll.

The reason why the fish you will see never get any bigger is because of the temperature of the water, which remains at a constant four degrees centigrade or thirty-six degrees Fahrenheit all the year round, regardless of climate changes around or above.

Nearly everyone is now looking forward to Lake Louise. You could almost feel the anticipation in the atmosphere, all of us knowing that the expected sighting and consequent cry would announce the winner. No such luck! For it was the chateau that first came into view, and then we failed to see anything as we all had to enter and walk through the hotel to glimpse "the Jewel of the Rockies". Nobody was disappointed; the weather was in our favour, most of us just stood there, overcome with the beauty of it all. Telling people about this experience has always been difficult, and now to describe it in print, I can only try to improve my description. From where we were standing, as you looked out across the lake you saw the Victoria Glacier in the very far background, then in the very foreground, right across the lake's surface, was its magnificent reflection. Then bearing down on either side, right to the end of the lake, were two mountain ranges looking as if a huge wedge-shape had been removed and transplanted with the Victoria Glacier. The photo that we took is one of my prize snaps! As you walked further down the lake on the pathways provided and looked back, what a size the hotel was! And especially as the sun had now climbed up over the distant mountains, we were reminded of why it is so named–Chateau Lake Louise.

Inside my hotel, my, what an interior! I thought the hotel at Banff was the bee's knees, but this hotel eclipses it–all the elegance of Victorian standards, the high ceilings, the decoration and again the attentions of the staff to your smallest request. Yes, indeed, "the Jewel of the Rockies".

Shortly after re-boarding the coach, Henry is telling us a lot about the past history of the Chateau. It was originally built in 1893, chiefly of wood, with brick fireplaces and load-bearing walls. This building was burnt down in 1924, then rebuilt and it remained unchanged until 1987, when a new wing was added, called the "Glacier Wing". This looks out onto the lake and glacier, giving spectacularly breathtaking sunrise views. You also have to remember that all of this is under twenty feet of snow during the winter months.

A mountain we have just passed by has its glacier shaped like a crow's foot. Again due to the melt of snow, it has lost three of its claws and is now known as "the two toed crow's foot glacier".

By now, Henry is in full swing with a history of the pioneers of his country. James Hectar, another Canadian Pacific Railway Surveyor, discovered "Kicking Horse Pass".

This was so named because one of his packhorses gave him an almighty kick on his backside. This is where the railroad and highway pass through to British Columbia.

Mosquito Lake passes us by as Henry tells us that you don't hang around there long, as it's frequented by hoards of the little monsters. This is one of many lakes that drains away in the fall to leave it empty.

The Bow Lake arrives, which has the Bow Glacier to thank for its attraction. Every one of us was taken aback by the colour of the water. Henry, ready for this gasp from us all, said, "I daresay you are wondering why the water is green? Well what happens, the glacier is always on the move, very slight, but never still. It's the movement of rocks against the rock walls that in turn scrapes off a fine powder, in fact like starch. It arrives on the lake but does not sink; it floats, reflecting the colour green." "Opaque of a Spectrum" are Henry's exact words. (I did make a note making sure and confirming this with Henry later.) "During the summer months, depending on how much melt is going on, this then reflects the rock powder's colour, either not particularly noticeable or very noticeable, as with the startling green you see today." No doubt the Bow Lake is proud of its glacier.

The Peyto Lake: Bill Peyto, another old trapper and timber-man, had this lake named after him. Quite an unusual man was Bill! He very much liked his own company. The story goes that not only was he earning a living by trapping animals, but also introducing visitors to the conditions that he worked in. A few now and then, being ardent listeners and watchers, considered this an easy way to make a living. What they did not reckon on was that Bill would notice this, then at nightfall he would make a fire for them all and provide wood supplies for them through the night. Then he would move a fair distance from them, light his own fire and settle down for the night, thus leaving them in a state of shock after a night of the sounds of the wilderness. In the morning, most, if not all, wanted to get back to Banff as quickly as possible. The cries of bears, wolves and other wild creatures had made them change their minds. On one occasion he captured a bobcat, one with a very short tail, and walking into a bar in Banff and seeing there were quite a few patrons in at the time, he released it. This promptly cleared the establishment in seconds; then, quickly retrieving the animal, he sat down to enjoy his glass in the solitude that he had come to enjoy.

We had now almost reached our destination, the Icefields, when Henry stopped the coach right beside a small area of dwarf fir trees. He asked, "Does anyone know why those spruce trees are so small?" No reply. "They are perfectly healthy trees, nothing wrong with them at all, but they only receive about eighty to ninety days of suitable growing conditions throughout the year. That makes for just a couple of centimetres, and they also produce cones and seed! Can you see the very tiny ones?– They are seedlings with ten years' growth."

Wonders will never cease!

Leaving the nice warmth of our coach after arriving some five minutes late at the Columbia Icefields, again we were in the company of several other tour parties. As Henry tells us, "It is a very popular tourist spot." I must say on my first view looking around I imagined it to be several ice rinks combined, with the sides the shape of large ice grandstands. Cold! You can write that again! I was glad I had put on my extra cardigan as the atmosphere around us was rapidly going downhill.

Our first transport was a Snocoach that took us partway over some pretty rough-going. Then we all got out and entered another one; this one was a monster with huge wheels that took us down a gradient of, I would say, a one in four drop of twenty feet. There were quite a few screams, but we were all well strapped in, soon at the bottom and now well out on the Icefield. The Snocoach driver said, "You can now get your ice legs. Be very careful how you walk, as it is very slippery, and be back here in twenty minutes."

It is going to be difficult to describe how I felt while I was here—certainly a sense of bewilderment at the size of the place, for never before had I seen so much ice collectively in my life, ever. Most of us were now walking about quite nonchalantly on what lay beneath us. There was, we were informed, 1,260 feet of solid ice underneath. Can you imagine that? I could not, nor several of our party. Coming into view was an old gentleman, and, looking at his dress, he appeared to be starting out on a walk. I walked beside him for a while and asked him, "Excuse me, but are you going far?" The reply was, "I hope to reach a good way up Mount Columbia," pointing with his stick in the direction of the mountain in front of us. I asked him, "How high is it?"

"It's about 11,235 feet above sea level, but I don't think I shall get very far, as the weather is going to break before long. I have done the climb many times. Now at seventy years of age, I do say to myself there is another day tomorrow."

He was not following any obvious pathway or track,

and now, as the surface was getting rough with deeper and deeper ice furrows all around us, I shook his hand, wished him luck and turned back.

The Icefield guide was beckoning to us all that he wanted us back on board the Snocoach, and through the window I spotted the old chap and noticed the progress he had made for, for now he was just a speck in the distance— the right equipment, good clothing, spiked boots and that proven companion, a walking stick. I am afraid it's not my cup of tea.

The guide was now telling us, as we made our way back, "Approximately twenty-three feet of snow falls here each winter. The melt of this Icefield drains into three oceans, the Pacific, the Arctic and the Atlantic.

"Canada has experienced four major 'Ice Ages', hence the formation of the Rocky Mountains around which formed part of an enormous ice sheet. This helped to grind and carve out the most recent one, which ended 10,000 years ago.

"The glaciers, as you are all aware by that sharp incline we have just climbed are now in retreat. This means that fifteen years ago that was the level of the Icefield!" There was a very loud gasp as he made that last statement.

Now in retreat, as the summer melt is far greater than the winter fall of snow, an Icefield is formed when snow that falls on peaks and plateaux accumulates each year with very little summer melt. When the snow attains a depth of 100 feet the bottom layers become pressurised into ice, more snow falls on top, and the depth of ice now increases, then overflowing into surrounding valleys. Then the melt may start, in some instances, great rivers. The Athabasca Glacier we are now on covers an area of two and half miles wide and about four and a half miles long, the depth as mentioned is 1,200 feet. The whole glacier is continually on the move, and gradually moving down from this Colombian Icefield. From the output of this Icefield and its companion glaciers is formed, as you know, a gigantic reservoir providing fresh clean water to hundreds of thousands of people here in Canada. It moderates local summer temperatures and increases the severity of the winter climates, profoundly impacting on the lives of the plants and animals in the area.

Icefields also provide our scientists with a frozen record of atmospheric and climatic conditions of past history and its life. They offer us an unbelievable glimpse of what North America looked like as the surface of the continent was being shaped tens of thousands of years ago, and perhaps in time—as equipment and science develops—maybe millions of years. We all thanked the driver for telling us all this. My own impression as I looked back out of the rear seat of Henry's coach was: "It was more than a bit special."

Henry continues in the same vein as the driver of the Snocoach: "Someday this will no longer exist, but that is centuries away."

The water from the Icefields is the purest water known to mankind and the water now melting from the ice was snow before the Industrial Revolution. As I am making a few notes, I realise how important this area is to preserve geographically and scientifically. There are so many reasons why we should protect this colossus of our heritage, and yet we aren't. Just one example of our neglect comes to mind as we are waiting to get back onto the highway with the burbling note of the engine ticking over: the gasses from the exhaust system and the damage they are doing collectively to the world's environment with their greenhouse effect. As this global warming bites more and more into the ozone layer (as one generation follows another) this splendiferous sight that I have witnessed today will some time be just another hillside, a table mountain with huge pine, fir and spruce forest abounding. What a terrible thought!

My companions, like me, seem to have been confounded by its cold, clear clinical beauty. Shortly after this we had a stopover, just off the main highway, I had a blueberry muffin which I am sure was the largest I think I have had the privilege to enjoy, together with a cuppa.

Following the Athabasca River to Jasper, was an experience in itself. Having left the Banff National Park, we were now travelling through the Jasper National Park. Seeing the river now and then round many bends, we noticed how low the water was in places, Rosanne did mention this over the mike— "that the white water rafting would be over for the season". Every now and again, you would see the boulders right across the river, so you had to agree. Driving on the outskirts of Jasper and following a narrow road, I for one wondered what Henry was about. Round a bend, we arrived at Maligne Lake. This was again a surprise for, except for a few pools of water scattered around, it was void of water.

We all vacated the coach, not only to stretch our legs, but to try to understand what Henry had told us before stepping out: "When the lake is full of water I would not have been able to park up the coach where it says 'Parking'." He then continued: "Earlier in the summer months the water from the lake comes right over and completely covers the road with several centimetres, and it's impassable as you are unable to locate the road."

I for one could not "fathom" this disappearing act and as we stood there, almost with one voice we asked, "Where does it go to, Henry?"

Henry: "In the summer months all the area you see now is covered with water. Then in the fall, which only occurred a few weeks ago, the total expanse drains away into subterranean channels following underwater courses which have been there for thousands of years, then going into tributaries that feed the main rivers." I together with my companions am sure that this is another unsung miracle, as Henry in his less-than-modest way puts the Maligne Lake into perspective. "It is a massive 'clean-up' operation without help or guidance from any authority in the country. Timbers, rubbish, decayed carcasses, any old four-wheelers, regardless of size, are all smashed, mangled, minced and split apart as they pass through the rock sieve, which forms a natural environment habitat."

Back on board, this time I transferred myself to the coach's nearside as we travelled back along the Maligne Canyon, so the river and its contents were quickly identifiable, and I was not to be disappointed. There were rocks and broken trees on my immediate left, the boulders as big as houses (this is no exaggeration) and forming grotesque formations. Henry explained, "Some of the rocks, the larger ones, have been swept down from places many miles away, Geologists have proved that some samples taken have no connection with this area at all. This is when you realise how powerful water is." I did mention this to Henry later on—"No, the final resting places are never certain, for when floods and torrents cascade down, those rocks are always on the move."

To the north of Jasper we stopped, after passing through some very narrow roads, at Pyramid Lake, in the shadow of Pyramid Mountain. It was nice to stretch our legs and a walk across a narrow bridge helped to get them going again! Back in the coach, we finally saw what most of us had been looking for all day–a bear; most of us saw its hindquarters and fewer still were quick enough to get a picture, including myself.

Another lake passed us by, this one Patricia Lake–as Henry tells us, a very good fishing one. Back into Jasper and our hotel the Lobstick Lodge, arriving at seven-thirty p.m. I don't mind telling you that we were all knackered after a busy day of snapping and sightseeing.

Day 6! One thing I seldom do when I am at home is oversleep, and after my first night's sleep here in Jasper there was no chance of my doing that here, as my bedroom window was on the same level as the road outside–just ten feet of lawn, and then the kerb of the road. Fully awake by six-thirty a.m. I experienced most of the early morning sunrise. Soon up and having a quick breakfast, by eight a.m. I was out and investigating the town. In daylight, I realised what a charming little township it was. Most of the streets I found had nice tidy properties with neat gardens back and front, with right behind them the pine, spruce and larch forest! In some instances, the forest was right in the back gardens, climbing forever upwards. I had not realised how near we were to the mountains.

I followed a road that led me to the Canadian National

Railway, and beyond this the Athabasca River. As I looked about me there was forest all round, and now I was aware that I was in one of the largest National Parks in the world. Checking on this when I got back to the Lobstick Lodge, I discovered it to be 10,878 square kilometres: "Phew!"

Several more of my party wished to visit the famous Whistler Mountain. On finding out that conditions were going to be in our favour, we knew this was a good start to the day. A ride by gondola took us almost to the summit (2,464 metres) and then a short walk to an observation turret gave us some superb views all round. This was not the top by any means as the footpaths continued for considerable distances, all upwards for several hundred metres. Seeing people on the skyline turning back proved that we were not at the end of the trail. A few of us on the lower slopes had found our own pathways to enjoy the scenery about us and below. We did take some rather unusual photos, not only of peaks and nearby mountains, but also of a small area of snow nearby whose occupants were causing us to walk very stealthily. For frolicking in the snow were about a dozen grouse, already with their winter plumage, and, my word, were they enjoying the conditions! It was now a nice bright sunny late autumn day, not unpleasant, comfortable.

Whistlers Mountain is so named because of the small rats or rodents (which we never saw) that inhabit it and whistle from their burrows (which we did see). Most of the party had some refreshment while we were here, and I know at the time I mentioned how the building we were sitting in only had a few concrete columns to support us. Nobody seemed to take much notice of this remark until, on the way down, my three companions said, "How precarious the cafeteria looks up there."

Returning to Jasper it was clear to see, as I had spotted from the top of Whistler Mountain, that this was a busy rail town with wagons the big word for business.

I was sitting on a seat beside the rail-track with John, whose wife and their friend Sheila had gone window shopping, when a wagon train went by at little more than walking pace. I said to John, "I counted over 100 wagons."

"Can't be," came the reply.

After some ten minutes another one came along and this time we both counted the wagons, and agreed there were 109. Shortly after this the whole lot came to a standstill, so stepping out beside one I said, "I think each one is over fifty feet long."

"If they are, I reckon the whole thing's a mile in length."

"I doubt it," says John, parting company and said, "See you later." On closer inspection of the wagons, each was loaded with granite chippings or something similar.

I decided to explore this side of Jasper a bit more, the west side. It did not matter where you put your nose—round each corner everything was clean and tidy and quiet. You did not realise how peaceful it was until a vehicle (heavy duty) passed by and then the silence returned. It was uncanny. I was walking past a Royal British Legion Club when a chap called out, "Do you want a drink? Come on in!"

"No thanks, but could I pop in later?"

"Yes of course you can."

Back at the hotel Rosa mentioned that a lot of snow had fallen a few miles away, the first of the winter fall in fact.

But don't worry: tomorrow we are travelling away from this and where we are heading, British Columbia, is much warmer. After a wash and brush-up and once I'd had my evening meal, I mentioned the invitation I had received from the nearby Legion Club to a few of the party. All declined

When I got there, I walked in to find some twenty or more people. I said to the young lady behind the bar that I was not a member. She replied, "Don't worry. Just sign the non-members book." Soon a very welcome pint arrived, then, just as I was sitting down, the chap who I had seen earlier came over and insisted that I join them at their table. After I had been introduced to the other nine people by Dave the good Samaritan, I soon began to see how educational this chance meeting was going to be.

My new-found friends were sitting round a splendid pine wood table, some fifteen feet long by eight feet wide and about two feet six inches high. The top was about three inches thick, the whole table in a dark, highly polished varnish, with huge comfortable chairs to match. It reminded me of old banqueting furniture of old England.

Dave, like all the others, was now retired. They had all been associated with the railways during their working life and I was proving to be the centre of their conversation, especially amongst their wives who were not entirely satisfied that I was from England. What county was I from? It seemed that everyone round the table, their parents, grandparents or even earlier relatives were from England originally. I told them I was from Essex. One had never heard of it. When I mentioned a few of the other counties it appeared that most of their relatives had come from up north, and only a couple kept in touch with relatives.

None had been to England, and as a chap called Bill said, "At our age it's most unlikely."

A game that was taking a lot of our dollars was Pontoon Tickets: each person purchased from the lady behind the bar a dollar's worth of tickets. The proceeds from the winning tickets would go into a central pool, and, when the glasses needed replenishing, the pool was tapped for funds. This proved most popular throughout the evening.

I said to Dave, "I was very curious about some of the trains and the amount of wagons they were pulling—they must have been a mile long!" I had several replies in an instant, including Dave's. "Some are 2½ miles long and each truck is 56.3 inches long and weighs 50 tonnes. The whole train sometimes weighs 14,000 tonnes. Yes, my job was a clerk so it was most important that I got all my weights and measures correct. Tom over there worked with George and Ken on engines, and every one of us started with steam. Now it's all diesel on the main lines." I asked him about what was in the trucks, as they appeared to be filled with granite chippings. "They could have been, but all around us there are vast deposits of coal, which are all in open-cast mines, by the mountain-load. Also potash, petroleum, cobalt, platinum, nickel, copper, zinc, lead and yes there's still gold about. Limestone by the mountain-load and if there's thousands of lakes there sure is thousands of mountains."

One of the wives then remarked, "The government has not got a clue, there are going to be elections shortly. Then we might be able to use some of our mineral wealth properly." The men all agreed that a lot of improvements could and should be made to everyone's household. I agreed by saying, "Yes, we have the same problems at home." It was unanimous all round, "home and away", that improvements along with a big pension increase were overdue.

A chap named Alf had joined us and was sitting a couple of chairs away. Overhearing his conversation, I gathered he was in the building trade, an impression reinforced when he said he had been screeding a floor today and he had to give it a fall of three-eighths of an inch, in a stretch of floor twenty feet long. On hearing this I quickly told him, "I did not realise that they worked in feet and inches over here in Canada, surely you do all your measurements using the metric system?"

"No, not on your nelly," they all said. "Feet and inches!"

Dave then told me that Jasper was so named after a Jasper Hawes who was in charge of the North West Trading Company post back in the early 1800s, dealing with trappers and their furs. Most of the animals that they hunted are still around today! Elk, mule deer, bighorn sheep, coyote, moose, lynx, cougars, ragged goats, caribou, beaver, bears, black, brown and grizzly and wolves. Although there are not many about, there are still pockets of them. The first railroad arrived in 1911 and a few hundred people decided to settle. Those early settlers had some rough winters to endure to get the place established, but they stuck at it and now the rewards are for everyone to see. The population is now 3,300 here in Jasper. In Canada there are 27,000,000 sharing some 3,800,000 square miles. "But what is important is that sixty-one per cent of us list our mother tongue as English."

"Do you know about the Canadian Shield?"

"No," I said, "what's that?" I was thinking it was a

trophy put up for ice hockey or similar. Was I glad I did not think my thoughts out loud, as Dave tells me that, "It's like a huge half-circle of ancient granite rock that covers half Canada! No, it's not in this part of Canada. It's laid out from the Arctic North of Labrador and Quebec in the east; it continues round the Hudson Bay shores of Ontario and Manitoba and then back up to the Arctic Islands of the North West Territories. Did you know that the state of Ontario is twice the size of France?"

"No I did not realise that."

It was now nearly eleven p.m. and I had just purchased a round for us all when Bill made a little speech and presented me with a souvenir. It was in the form of a blue ribbon stating that I had been a guest of the Jasper Legion Branch 31 and then in gold capitals, "GEM OF THE ROCKIES".

I thanked them all for their kindness and hospitality and bade them all goodbye. Dave said, "I am going past the Lobstick. I'll walk along with you."

I was grateful that no vehicle was involved as outside it was snowing. Wherever you looked, the snow had covered everything in a remarkably short time, the pine, spruce and the lamp standards; as we passed them, they all had a Xmas card effect. In fact, as we walked along, I remarked to Dave, "How warm it is with the amount of snow that's fallen; I expected it to be freezing."

His reply: "This is the beauty of this climate, it is very gradual when the cold weather begins to set in, when it's about fifteen degrees below on a regular basis you are certainly cold, but your body has acclimatised itself to the conditions, so it is not too bad."

Day 7! I had partially closed the bedroom curtains, but not fully, so the light appeared through a chink. Looking outside I discovered it was still snowing up and down the street, now under a white blanket. By the time we had had breakfast, packed our bags and waited for Henry to come along, the snowfall was light, and this was melting as soon as it hit the road surface. I said to Henry, "Have the gritting lorries been out and about?"

"Yes," and a nod came by way of reply. He had now decided to reverse the coach directly under the large overhanging roof that formed part of the Lobstick's entrance. This he did with much applause from everyone, as no one got wet, the snow had now turned to rain and not even a suitcase got wet either.

All the time-pieces needed to be reset by one hour, because British Columbia time is one hour behind Alberta, the state we were now leaving.

Highway 16...to Prince George. A stop after about half an hour to see the Yellow Head Pass, 3,760 feet high, and here one of the company took my camera and captured a very friendly Stella Jay who was trying to remove my shoelaces–it apparently is quite common in these parts. Back in the coach, Henry tells us that the Yellow Head Highway we are now travelling on is the longest in the world! Some 11,000 miles.

Next stop is the Mount Robson Park, which is overshadowed by Mount Robson itself, towering above us, 4,000 metres or 12,992 feet. Rosanne tells us that we are very lucky this morning as it is nearly always covered in cloud. One person she knew had been coming here on and off for seventeen years, and in all that time had never seen the peak once. As we all stepped out of the coach and walked round the other side, there it was in all its morning glory! It was just waiting for all those cameras from some eight coaches to break into action. Rosanne calls out, "Hurry there's a huge cloud arriving," and within less than five minutes of her saying that, there is nothing! One tour group that we kept bumping into was a party from Wales, one of whom was Dai and his family with whom I had already shared a glass or two. He came towards me, and said, "Where is it, Boyo?" I was not sure myself now, as I was finding it difficult even to see where the base started. However, pointing in the general direction of where I thought it might be, I replied, "I am quite sure it is above those pines." Now raining steadily, I must say if I had been with the Welsh party I would have felt just as demoralised and dejected as them. I assured them, "You have got to be quick with your camera," and then looking up to where I thought it might be, there was suddenly a patch of blue, the snow-capped summit. Then it was gone. One of his party said, "I got it." I should think one of the most disappointed photographers was the one who had collected all his equipment from a coach, came along loaded down with it all and had no luck at all. As he said, "We are only allowed a limited time here so we shall have to come back another year."

Seeing Rosanne waving to us, it was clearly time to depart. Henry is now in top form as first we have to be observant on one side then as quick as a flash, on the other. Nearly everyone saw the moose that was on the near side as it dashed through a clearing in the forest. There was not much chance of seeing at close quarters the place where the Red Indians drove the buffalo over the cliff. This indeed must have been arranged and carried out with great skill, as Henry describes this centuries-old method of hunting this proud beast for the benefit of the whole tribe. What I did notice as we travelled more into British Columbia, were the number of fir forests, ranging either side of the highway, up to the top of mountains, down into valleys—continuous and endless.

Our break came at noon, this time a stop at a log-cabin type of diner, which sustained us all with some home-cooked goodies of excellent quality. A few of the company are still with English time, and they tell me that we are now eight hours behind English time.

We arrived at our destination, Prince George, at five-thirty p.m. My room overlooked a large part of the commercial side of the town. It was true what Henry had told us: "Timber is big business," for I could see all around, paper and timber mills in abundance.

Last but not least that day, an evening meal with Jean, Rosanne and Henry—very enjoyable.

Day 8! All up, packed, quick cuppa and ready to depart by six a.m. We all thanked Henry for his splendid skill in selling his country to us in such an unforgettable manner, then all chipping in with several dollars each to show our appreciation, we bade our farewells to him at the railway station.

Today we have been assured by Rosanne is one we will not forget as long as we live. It is an all-day train ride through the Rockies to Vancouver. The rail company are also providing three meals and any information required.

The train left at seven-twenty a.m.—nice roomy carriages with plenty of glass for observation. I had hardly settled down when the breakfast menu arrived. From the moment the train left the station, the conductor made it his business to walk through the carriages and chat to us all. Without a doubt Tom Deverall was different.

"Make sure you are on the right side of the train to see the ospreys on their nests." And lo and behold, twelve telegraph poles, and balanced at the top of each one a nest! Presumably, the wires had long gone, and as Tom tells us, very seldom is there an accident where the nest falls off. Each year every nest has successful results. We saw three birds hovering around; to my mind, though, they did look weird.

Quesnal, Williams Lake and Clinton all seemed to be following like us the mighty Fraser River, Creeks, gullies, mountains, ravines and canyons passed us by, and now and again we would slow down because of an overnight rock-fall. Men would be clearing our safe passage through, enabling us to proceed without stopping. In no time lunch was being served and as you might guess salmon was on the menu. My word! How it was presented and placed in front of us to enjoy the exquisite grandeur that surrounded it. Of course, the photographers were having a field day, especially John who was shooting everything with his camcorder.

A stop at Lillooet for forty-five minutes to stretch our legs and also for a change of crew for the train. Our new conductor, Dick Schauler, is just as pleasant and helpful as Tom Deverall. As soon as the train started rolling again, we all had excellent treatment, each of us being made to feel the most important person on board. You could move from one end of the train to the other, meeting and chatting to all nations' natives.

Dick had told us that soon we would be crossing the

Fraser River Canyon if anyone would like to take photos from the rear coach. "*Now's* your opportunity." The driver, on instruction from Dick no doubt, stopped the train right in the centre of the bridge and there I was, with· many others, snapping away, left and right. Recalling it to others quite a few times surprises even myself, as never at any time in my life have I been afraid of heights! But here in the middle of that bridge looking down hundreds of feet to the mighty Fraser River on just a single rail track, maybe seven to eight feet wide with "only a 2.09 foot high guard-rail" on either side. And those guard-rails certainly looked fragile.

This was to me nerve-tingling, heart-stopping, and set the pulses racing. I'm sure if anyone had screamed I would have flung myself to the floor! Everything had stopped; the silence was just deathly. It seemed as though time had not accepted modern times here. Then, breaking the solitude, "Toot-toot" from the front, and we were rolling again. I mentioned how my temperature was rising when we were out there sitting still in the middle of that bridge to my companions at the time. They replied, "You are getting old, Perc." Perhaps they were right, but I can assure you I was mighty glad to get to the other side of that bridge.

By late afternoon, we had dropped down from the high Rockies to where a small tributary of the Fraser River had travelled beside us for quite some time. Dick called out, "The salmon are spawning on the right hand side of the train. All those folk who are sitting on the left–if you don't move over you will not see this wonderful spectacle of nature again." Then you will never guess–the whole train came to a halt so everybody could witness the whole event. It moved along a bit more so the carriages further back could be satisfied too. Then underway again, Dick over the intercom asked, "Is every person contented now?"

A big cry rang out through the carriages, "Thank you, yes."

Walking through the train, it was surprising to me the number of passengers who were using camcorders, and, so far, the weather had been kind to them all. Spotting Dick, I started chatting to him. He told me that he was retiring shortly and then he would be able to devote more time to his lifelong passion, fishing. Was I a fisherman, he asked? "No not likely! I always admire people who stick it out in all sorts of foul weather." Dick now realising that there were quite a few people listening in then told us a bit more about the salmon. "I never stop admiring those Pacific ones who leave their ocean to swim hundreds of kilometres up the rivers to spawn, Sockeye, Coho, Chinook. They mate, lay their eggs, yet less than fifty per cent return to the ocean. The eggs hatch, the offspring staying in the rivers for a couple of years. The ocean calls them, and they remain there for perhaps five years. Then 'home' calls them, so they migrate back to the place we have recently passed to mate and then to begin the cycle once more."

"Marvellous," I said.

I am unable to describe his voice as accurately as I would like, but if I were to suggest a polite Canadian deep growl then that would give you the flavour and I'm sure would not offend him. I thought this would be a good opportunity to ask him if I could have a word with the train driver and have a look round his cabin. The reply: "Sure, follow me."

I was introduced to the driver and his mate. First, I let them know that I had a tape recorder: "Would you mind if I kept the mike on while we're talking, and do you think you could let me have a few toots?"

"Yes of course, do you want bells as well?"

I was highly delighted, as I received a volume of bells and toot-toots every now and again as we chatted. Both had been involved with the Rockies Run for several years and yes, they loved their jobs. As the co-driver remarked, "You don't know what's round the next bend," and I could not agree more. At the time, we were running along a lower level with very little straight track ahead of us. The close proximity of the rock walls was surprising, while the trees at times appeared to be almost shaking our hands, as if wanting to bid us a safe journey. Around each corner we would enter another tunnel, then there would be a short section of sunlight and a patch of sky between overhanging rocks, this usually accompanied by blasts on the hooter. As Pete remarked, "It's done mainly to warn the animals that we are approaching." There was nothing special about their cabin, small and compact, it included very tiny seats. While I was with them there was no time for either driver to use them as both were very much occupied in keeping a beady eye open.

I was very surprised and touched when the co-driver Larry said to me, "Will you accept this souvenir brooch on behalf of the company?"

My word! It certainly is special; it has the words "B.C.Rail" inscribed on it. I said, "I'm most grateful for this and will treasure it for a long time, together with your splendid company and my time here in the cabin with you both." I shook their hands and opened the door to the first coach. As soon as I entered a voice called out, "What were you doing in there, boyo?" The Welsh contingent from the rival company! I tried to explain to them, that I was not at all interested in the train driver's job, but was just fulfilling another ambition of mine "to steer a train". One said, "What was all the tooting and bells in aid of?"

I replied, "Certainly they were for my benefit, as I have this tape recorder taping all conversations and noises. In fact, it's even recording us right now. The toots and bells are also to frighten away animals from tunnel entrances and exits. Cheerio, all the best."

Dusk was just beginning to arrive as I made my way back to the coach and seat. Jean, my companion for most of the journey, was like myself a wandering enthusiast and both of us arrived back to find our evening meal prepared and ready. I am quite sure that she cannot make head nor tail of me. Certainly, educational differences stood out a mile, but as usual I found this was not a barrier to enjoying each other's company. Of course, we had our own opinions on various subjects whilst we were in conversation, and, invariably, as this became more apparent to me that it was wise to change the subject, I would draw Jean's attention to the window: "Have a look at that."

Salmon again on the menu if you wanted it! Both of us enjoyed it first time round and we did so again, this time even more luxuriously presented than before, the whole made more comfortable by two bottles of excellent wine. After our meal, I quietly took out my "Rockies" pamphlet. I must say I did not realise how important some of the places we had passed through had been in their connections to the history of Canada. Quesnal was the place where the gold rush of the 1860s was—"the pioneering place of gold in them there hills".

Gold Fever brought many settlers to this region. Over millions of years ago, glaciers had ground out veins of gold in the mountains; then torrential rains and landslides washed the heavy nuggets, grains, flakes and dust into the river sand and gravel bottoms. There it lay until the Red Indians started bartering it at the trading posts for whatever was worthwhile in exchange. Whisky was the chief appetiser. But the gold did not last long, just over twenty years. Through those years there were plenty of pioneers who decided that there was more than gold here—fur, timber, the job of building railroads. Ranchers, frontiersmen and adventurers had travelled long distances, and then decided to call the place home. Whistler, Squamish! In the latter, there is "Loggers' Sports Day". I bet that is pretty popular, for they come from miles away (hundreds in some cases), for anything to do with logs. Then there is a caribou marathon, and a spud festival in another town. I wonder what went on there!

I do know something, as our train pulled into Vancouver Station, everybody I spoke to had enjoyed the 462 miles of extraordinary railroading. It had given all of us an experience that was not going to be easily forgotten! It was a trip that had been made all the more pleasant for us because the weather had, from the moment we had boarded to when we were now alighting, been in our favour. I searched out Dick and, shaking his hand, thanked him for all the knowledge that he had so helpfully passed on to us, and especially for stopping the train, and letting us see for ourselves the salmon spawning at their journey's end. His answer: "I sure am proud that my company and I have been able to give you all a few of our country's delights."

"One question," I asked. "This has worried me for some time: does the service travel through the winter months? Only we have heard of twenty feet of snow in some parts."

Dick's reply: "Conditions have to be very bad to stop us from carrying out our schedules. Occasionally the snow is three to four metres high! The snowplough blasts it away in no time and very few times do we arrive less than ten minutes either side of the arrival clock."

I quickly pointed out to him, "But the bridge over the Fraser Canyon?"

"That's nothing; with the hi-tech equipment that the boys use now, they are clear in no time. They know that if there are any hold-ups, they stop everything that needs conveying from one side of the Rockies to the other."

The time was now eight-forty-five and quite dark.

"The coach is this way, Percy," I heard Rosa say. Getting in the coach the driver had quite a long look at our luggage and then, casting a glance in our direction, I'm sure his thoughts must have been, "Why all this baggage for so few people?"

Everywhere you looked, the city was lit up like a fairyland. I said to Rosa, "Is there a festival or something on here in Vancouver? They don't seem to mind the expense of lighting up the place."

"No," came the reply. "This is the usual display, you wait till you see the hotel."

My! When we arrived, it excelled everyone's ideas about spending money to please the customer. It was another "Far East" acquisition, which, as Rosa tells us, has had major changes made to it over the last three years. Now completed it has only been open one month.

I must say at once that the foyer was big, bold and beautiful. The architect, no doubt with the twenty-first century in mind, had planned this to perfection. Not only were the decorations in tune with the upholstery and ornamentation, but all was co-ordinated with the décor on the lift, exits and any other doors. We were made to feel just like "Lords and Ladies" during our stay. The mirrors had a whole lot to do with the buzz I got when in the foyer. From the entrance doors, they went right round from floor to ceiling–giant pieces fifteen feet or more in length. The joints in the verticals were a job to see with the naked eye. I honestly could not get used to them. If I came up from the basement restaurant, then any of the three lifts I was aiming for, behind me, in front of me or overhead, the mirrors were there. During our stay here, I went several times to the staircase to find it was directly behind me! Fortunately, the concierge would wave his or her hand to warn me! As I told them, "I've never experienced anything like this–'using mirrors in place of wallpaper'." That first night I went to bed as tired out as if I had walked over the Rockies, instead of being conveyed so luxuriantly and in such splendid and capable hands.

Day 9! Jean, today's companion, had told me she had a cold and would not be moving far, so I decided to find out more about Vancouver. I followed Rosa's advice and walked down to find the skytrain. I had my map, and not until I had covered a fair distance and made some inquiries, were my worst fears confirmed: I'd gone in the wrong direction.

I purchased a ticket when I found a machine that sold the one I needed. It cost 2.25 dollars. This proved to be one of the cheapest one-day travel cards I have ever purchased. The skytrain had something like twenty-two stations, this being only my second experience of sitting in a computer-controlled train! No driver, no conductor and no noise—just magic. (My first trip on one of these was a few years ago on the Docklands Light Railway!) I went to the end of the stations shown on the map and then back again, at times going over high buildings and bridges. I was halfway there on my third journey and had been chatting to a fellow passenger when she asked, "Have you been to the Grouse Mountain?"

"No," came my reply. "Where's that?"

"Over there in North Vancouver! You have to get out here for the ferry crossing."

Thanking her, I alighted and made my way down to the ferry, joining the forty or so people who were waiting for its arrival. I saw a uniformed official and showed him my ticket. He said, "That one will take you there and back as many times as you like. The next one is in about ten minutes." It did not take long for it to arrive, me to board and subsequently alight on Lonsdale Quay—a matter of twenty minutes. Most of it was a covered market with umpteen stalls all filled with goodies, but what did take me by surprise was how everywhere was so clean and tidy with not a crumb of paper in sight.

A fish stall had drawn my attention on the way in, so on the way out I had a good look at its wares! Salmon! "All fresh," the young lady said. "Would you like to purchase one, Sir?"

"No," I said, "I am not into eating that sort of meal, but

do you think I could take a photo of you holding one?" I pointed to one of the bigger ones.

"Yes, certainly," she replied, picking up a monster.

The photograph taken, I asked her, "How much does it weigh?"

"Fifteen pounds–it was only caught yesterday. All the fishermen had a good catch, the biggest one weighed in at nineteen pounds."

I thanked her and promised her when the photo came out I would send her one.

The second floor of a restaurant was my next port of call as it was quite some time since I had had anything to eat or drink, the time now one p.m. Sitting near my table was a person in a blue uniform who I immediately thought was involved with bus transport so I asked her, "Where can I find the bus that takes me to the Grouse Mountain?"

The reply: "It's just round the corner, the bus terminal; it takes you direct and leaves in about fifteen minutes." I thanked her and was soon on my way.

The bus I wanted was preparing to leave. Hopping on board I showed the driver my ticket, who punched a hole in it and handed it back to me. I thought at the time, "I wonder when this ticket blows it!" Well, it did at the last stop, but only temporarily. I found I had to pay 12.50 dollars to have a ride up and down in a gondola. I still considered it a pretty cheap day's excursion so far for what I'd paid. The gondola must have held thirty or more people. Getting out at the completion of the gondola's journey, the next paret of the trip involved reaching the summit using a lift on a single-seater ski chair. On the way up this last section, I spotted coming down, and guessed correctly, an English couple. I called out, "Good afternoon."

The reply: "It's quite misty at the top."

Then looking further up the line of chairs, I could see nothing. I was travelling through clouds with only my lightweight jacket on. Nearing the stop point I called out, "Is anyone there?" in a voice loud and clear.

"No," a voice came back, at the same time as two hands grabbed me, undoing the safety harness that had held me in securely.

Looking round I said, "I think I will go down again and wait until the weather breaks."

The chap answered, "Sure, mate, go up and down as long as you like."

Another fifteen minutes and I was back up again. This time though the sun had come out and almost as far as the eye could see the mist had cleared up and visibility was now such that I could see in every direction around me— the Rocky Mountains spreading their formations well into America, with snow-capped peaks informing you of their positions. Asking the time, I was told three-thirty p.m., and, thanking the chaps, I caught the next one down, then the big lift and very soon I was back to ground level. The bus was ready to leave, so I jumped on. Lo and behold! Sitting next to me were the English couple, who were also going back to Lonsdale Quay. We were soon talking to each other and I for one quickly realised that they spoke my sort of language, so I said, "I have a feeling you are from my neck of the woods."

"Enfield," came the reply.

"Where are you from?"

"High Beech," they both said. "We used to do our courting there."

"What part of Enfield are you from?"

"Along the Ridgeway."

I continued, "I was in the building trade for quite a number of years and worked for a sub-contract bricklayer in that area. We built about twelve properties, three turnings on the left as you leave Windmill Hill, heading for Potters Bar! It was a cul-de-sac."

Looking at each other both said, "We live in that little estate! Well I never, and it still is a cul-de-sac."

Arriving at the bus terminus, we shook each other's hands and telling them exactly where I lived, they promised to look me up when they got the chance.

By now as I stepped off the bus and boarded the ferry, the sun was rapidly sinking in the west. By the time I arrived at the ferry terminal, it didn't look the same place that I had left a few hours earlier. It was dark now, and Rosa had drummed it into us all to make sure we were not in the Downtown Area after dark, and, if you were, to get out as quick as you can! I jumped on the first bus that came along, only to find the driver changing the destination, Stanley Park, to somewhere else. I waited at the bus stop for only a short while, then the right one came along. I jumped on board, showed him my ticket and asked, "Could you put me off at Stanley Park?"

Guessing correctly that I was not sure where I was staying, he said, "What's the name of your hotel, chum? I'll drop you as near as I can to it." For the life of me I could not remember, so getting near where the main group of hotels was, he stopped at a bus stop, and said, "In that direction," pointing.

Walking down the street I noticed several people walking on the other side, one of whom was a person in our party walking along, clutching a bottle. She quickly recognised me, saying, "I have just come from the off-licence."

"Are you going back to the hotel?" I inquired. "What's the name of the hotel?" I followed up more humbly.

"Yes I am," she replied. "You are a fool! Look up there, see that little squiggle, that's the Coast Plaza!"

"Thank you."

Funny! I had been looking at the sign on that particular hotel for some time, even when I was on board the ferry, thinking what a superb building it was with its illuminated sign! And now as we were strolling along, crossing the roads to get to it, I looked up and was sure the "squiggle" was laughing its head off! Nearing the hotel and looking through the avenue of trees that surrounded it, it appeared to be as bright a star as one in the heavens, many moons away with its bright blue background. The more you looked at it the more you were dazzled by its splendour.

Back inside the glowing interior I thanked Beryl and retired gracefully to my room.

Day 10! Sometimes recalling today, Saturday 9th October, I'm amazed that so many occurrences could occur in a single day. I was off to a flying start! As I mislaid my key to the bedroom, I searched high and low for it without success—the entire contents of the suitcase, even the lining, but no luck. Finally, I gave up, and went down the stairs to find Rosa. "Last one, Percy, where have you been?"

"I have lost the room keys."

"Oh don't worry about them, get on the coach."

A quick count round the party: it was well supported with some twenty-six on board. Our driver was from

Vancouver and made sure we all had a good education with regard to his city. Unfortunately, his voice did not gel with me at all. Mind you, it was quite interesting how he was describing everything about its history and its people.

Vancouver Island is the place we are to visit today. According to Rosa, the capital, Victoria, is a bit special as the climate there is so different to anywhere else in Canada.

On the way to catch the ferry to take us over, we passed through mile after mile of market garden. Our driver informs us this is the Fraser River Delta, and some of the most fertile soil in the world, the produce being sold not only in the island but also to Canada and world-wide as well.

We caught the ten a.m. ferry, the weather again in our favour as we docked an hour later, together with several coaches that were also destined for the Butchart Gardens like ourselves. The driver was now telling us what to expect to find in the Butchart Gardens and then, when he had finally told us to enjoy it, Rosa surprised him, and us too, with the knowledge that she had acquired over several visits. She told us how the gardens first came about and what was special about them. It was back in 1904 that the concept of the gardens was set out. In those days, the area was an old worked-out quarry. When the owners put it up for sale, Mr & Mrs Butchart saw its possibilities and decided to turn it into something special. This was then the start of a family commitment to give pleasure and enjoyment to hundreds of thousands of people across the world, giving all who visit the chance to see flowers in bloom all the year round, and most of them out of season. This has now spanned eighty years.

Asked if she knew the family her reply was, "Yes of course. I know the son very well. He is now an old gentleman in his eighties."

The driver now pulling into the car park, Rosa continues, "Generally he takes his turn in supervising the parking of coaches and cars, but I cannot see him around. We have not long here so be back here at one-thirty p.m. As there is fifty acres you will not see half! Good sign-posting is around, so you can take your pick where you want to go."

The layouts of some of the plots, borders, pools, etc., blended in so easily with their immediate surroundings that if we had not been informed that it was an old worked-out mine you would never suspect all the stone round us was natural and not artificial! I should imagine purpose-made is taboo round here. As I walked through taking photos, I had to admire the thought and consideration that is given to each successive bed or planting area. Here before my very eyes the bedding annuals looked as though it was the height of summer and not the advancing months of winter. There was not one but many beds of petunias, aster, salvia, all varieties of marigolds and many others with not a dead-head among them. There were a few members of the staff about to answer questions; it seemed that an army of working personnel arrive after the last visitor leaves, then tidy up, prick up the borders and beds, trim, edge, cut back whatever and chiefly replenish where ever they need to.

All the plants in the garden are nurtured. Grown somewhere else in different temperatures and then transported and transplanted en-bloc!—into their display and final abode, perhaps to give two or three months of consistency. Here the borders could be one variety and colour one day and overnight a complete change, with all the plants removed, dug over and replenished with good organic material and then perhaps, different species and coloration.

It did not matter where I walked, there were nice sensible paths with well manicured lawn between them and the beds. Even the herbaceous borders, the dahlia beds, the pelargonium beds were all as if they were planted yesterday, not a seed head forming, or for that matter a weed to be found! Of one of the staff nearby, I asked, "Where are all the weeds?" The reply: "They are about, sir; we try to make life difficult for them to survive; we like to catch them before they hatch."

You could see where various features had been added through the years, including the spectacular fountains, their ornamentals a bit special.

The natural rock faces that peeped through here and there had mostly been complemented with creepers of many varieties and now in the middle of the fall the foliage was doing the business for the snappers. I must admit this was planting of the highest standard. At the time, I did not think this colour scheme would be surpassed later in the day.

Back in the coach, a couple from Surrey had heard that I had collected two souvenirs from the Jasper British Legion and British Columbia Rail: would I accept a third one? This time it was a souvenir brooch of the Butchart Gardens. I accepted this and thanked them. I then brought out the other two and they were passed round the coach, with quite a lot of "They are jolly nice!"

The driver now tells us, "We are going for a drive

round part of the island that will be very interesting to you all."

I must say that this drive was indeed something special. The coastal road that we were travelling along had for part of the time not only powerful views on the seaward side, but also on the land side. We came to a place that the driver said was called Millionaires Row. He assured us that on entering this area cameras hidden in the branches of trees we were passing under were tracking our every move. I cannot remember a road layout scheme like the one we were passing through. Junctions were never parallel with each other. Roads did not continue for any length, then we turned to the left and then immediately to the right; some roads were much narrower than others. As Fred our driver informed us, "The properties here are like miniature palaces and each one with grounds like a mini Butchart Gardens." He also gave us a good description of some of the owners, their business and how many vehicles they had "stabled". Then as we moved back into Victoria itself you could not help but admire the old-fashioned lamp standards, each one adorned with hanging baskets of immense proportions! I am sure that Geoff Hamilton would have said, "Well, I'll take my hat off to every one of them."

It was three-fifteen p.m. when we arrived back in Main Street, and five p.m. was, I believe, mentioned as the time to be back on the coach.

Jean and I agreed to look at the Arts Theatre and the Natural History Museum. After walking for some fifteen minutes, we both realised this was not the right direction for either, so, turning back, Jean carried on to the theatre and I went into the Natural History Museum. Rosa had said, "It's well worth a visit." Absorbing, intriguing and riveting! That was how I found every floor. The ticket-holder had excellent viewing facilities, even a wheel-chaired visitor; nothing was left off the architect's drawing board.

Back in time to the pioneer days of Canada! We soon knew what they ate, where they lived–nothing was left out. As you passed by each section, you felt part and parcel of their everyday life.

I was gazing intently into and through a very large plate glass window when a voice said, "What is grabbing your attention, Percy?" It was Rosa.

I replied, "Look at those three dishes of raspberries."

"Well, what's different about them?"

I said, "Look at the name–'Salmon Berry'."

"It's still a raspberry of course," was her reply and she walked off.

I don't mind telling you I was knocked for six.

The three dishes contained raspberries of different colouring–all shades of pink, yellow, some almost white with just a hint of red in them. I had to convince myself that they were indeed artificial and only imitation berries. This fruit was a seasonal part of the regular diet of the Red Indians circa 1800s and wait for this, its Latin name was *Rubus Spectabile*. I don't think if I searched the whole building I would have found a more appropriate name for a specimen. It was a name perfect to fit a Queen's honours list.

Now this fruit has, I am sure, been lost over time; but what pleasure this fruit would have given flower arrangers and the like up and down the country. I did wonder at the time if this was their true colouring, but I have been able to find out nothing then nor since.

As I wandered round you seemed not only to educate yourself quite quickly with the knowledge that was so readily available, but to feel you were part of whichever theme you were looking at, especially with all the illustrations that were there to guide you. And if you were still not clear about something then there was always a smart uniformed steward to help with your enquiries.

I went into the section displaying totem poles; there were about a dozen of varying heights, widths and designs with what history each one has. To me, a real layman if ever there was one to grace this esteemed building, they were either unpleasantly evil, or pleasantly cheerful. When I remarked at their gloating, ogling, staring and leering faces, the lady steward really gave me some medicine chat, telling me, "You should never think of the Red Indians as being savages."

"The carvers of the totem poles treated them as objects of beauty, like you would observe your stately homes in England."

I said, "I fail to see that there is any comparison at all."

Didn't she give me the knowledge then and not from the book she was holding! "In fact they are better than the architects who designed those stately homes; they not only planned them but also did the work themselves, these savage Red Indians only had tools that were passed down through hundreds upon hundreds of years, and those skills passed from one generation to the next. The tree was cut down, roughly shaped, taken to its final position, completed, and painted and I might remind you that some paint has been proved to be over one thousand years of age, so you can see it was no rubbish they used. At the top of each totem was a figure of some design. If it was an animal, say a wolf, then the whole tribe would refrain from killing and eating it. There was months of hard work done on the totem to make it as lifelike as possible. Finally it would be raised into position and while it remained so the particular tribe would enjoy heath, prosperity and good hunting."

I must say she was a mine of information. I asked her, "How tall do you think this one was?" pointing to one that had been cut down, owing to ceiling restrictions. "About fifteen metres?"

"You must be joking." came the quick reply. "That one would have been more than forty metres high." And spreading her arms out as far as they would go, "–And this wide."

"That's more than 120 feet."

Now looking up to the ceiling height of ten metres, I could not put this into perspective until she said, "This one originally had a variety of carvings taken from nature from the base to its headpiece so you can see why each one was treated like a God."

"Whew!" Thanking her, I added, "Can you take a photo of me standing beside this one?"

"No, you must not go through the ropes, but I will take you with the totem in the background."

This accomplished I asked, "Is this hollow?"

"Yes, not all are; some are and some are not." Of those twelve on display, seven were hollow!

"You could have fooled me."

I thanked her most kindly and her parting words were, "We will be pleased to see you any time again, sir!"

I decided I would find out more about totems after I had had a cup of tea. I wanted to find Thunderbird Park.

This was located just behind the museum and there evidently they have a carving shed that contains totem poles. These are in several stages of production, some in their raw state with nothing done to them at all, others being carved and a number that were finished, painted and ready for ceremonial occasions.

I was crossing a large expanse of paving slabs, heading for the restaurant, when I just happened to glance across to a coach parked up nearby and with a lot of people inside waving. Then a woman came running over shouting, "Where have you been? We've been waiting twenty minutes and it's doubtful now if we make the ferry."

I stepped aboard the coach. Rosa said, "You will be in trouble, Percy, if we miss the ferry."

I said, "Sorry, am I the last?"

Then over the Tannoy she says, "And he has the bloody sauce to say, 'Am I the last?!' "

I wanted to get down the coach as far as possible and hide my head. The General and the Colonel (who I had nicknamed early on due to their military chatter and bearings) both put their feet up across the aisle so thwarting my progress.

I saluted them both and then heard them say in unison, "Court martial at eleven in the morning, do you agree?"

"Yes," I said.

"And so you should."

"And I'm sorry for making us late!"

The driver was now getting in on my misfortune and really stirring it up.

"If we miss the ferry it will be another two hours or more before the next one is due to leave the island. Added to which, as we near the ferry terminal private cars are a nightmare for they are all trying to get to the front so as to be able to get off first..."

You can imagine the atmosphere in the coach. I felt like the chief offender and was surrounded by the complete entourage of judge, jury and witnesses, all knowing what the verdict would be. In fact, the idle happy chatter had long gone, each person, like myself, was willing the driver to be more daring with the coach, willing to change the inevitable rush-hour traffic as thirty pairs of eyes glued themselves on the clock above the driver's head. "Stop, go, stop, go!" It made not the slightest difference. I could see the anxious ones looking at me as I hopped around the plentiful spare seats. I was never in the same one as I moved from side to side, thus making it difficult for them to spot and give me a glare.

We made it with plenty of time to spare. It was obvious that we were not going to be where the driver wanted us to be, right at the head of the queue, but we were only four coaches down. After we had stepped off the coach, making sure that I was the last, Rosa was waiting. Before she had a chance to say anything I said, "I'm very sorry, Rosa, for letting you down like that."

"Percy, please do not do that again. I know you don't have a watch, but why didn't you ask the time whilst you were in the museum?"

"I did."

"You knew what time you had to meet the coach."

"Yes."

"Don't do it again."

As I had hardly any food at all during the day I quickly found the cafeteria and with my tray I followed in the footsteps of Beryl, the lady who had found me the other evening. She turned round, saw it was me, "yours truly" standing behind her and said, "I am not talking to you."

"Why not? What have I done?"

"What have you done? You have not got a watch, you cannot read a map and most of the time you do not know where you are and you have upset Rosanne and all of us in the party. I for one am finished with you and don't wish to talk to you again."

I said, "Right-oh."

Within three minutes of this mini-explosion she arrived at the cashier desk with her tray of teas and cakes. Realising that she had insufficient money to pay for her purchases, and seeing her husband or whoever was quite a distance away, she turned round to me and said, "Percy, will you be kind enough to lend me two dollars until later?"

I duly obliged...thinking...

What a wonderful trip back to Vancouver this was going to be!

The sun was now sinking deep into the west. At times as we passed through so many islands we lost sight of it at times until it finally disappeared altogether. With its final disappearance, it gave an ethereal psychedelic sunset that offered us all a whole new perspective on the wonders of nature that were passing us by—seals, otters, wildfowl of many kinds and fishing boats all taking on hues that beggared belief. I am sure I have seen equally good sunset mixtures, but I'm positive, though, that this was one of the better ones, as our ferry tracked homeward—with the snappers saying, "Why does it have to end?"

Our instructions earlier from Rosa were, "Make sure you are all in the coach ready for a smart getaway."

I had been talking to a couple from Norfolk, Les and Joan who said to me they were going to make their way to the coach. I said, "Fair enough; I'll come with you." As we arrived back at the coach, it was unlocked so we stepped aboard. Back at our seats, I noticed them both whispering together and then Les said to me, "Just for a laugh, duck down in your seat."

"Yes why not?" I replied.

Rosa was the last one on and Les sitting opposite me said, "She's having a good look round"

Then..."Where is he this time?"

Both the general and the colonel said in unison, "He's frightened to face the court martial we had planned for him tomorrow."

I popped up from my seat and called, "Here I am," looking directly at Rosa. I am sure that a faint smile had started to appear as she said, "I'm glad you are." I thought at the time and still do, what a super person to put up with me.

Day 11! Sunday, a leisure day. Most everybody seemed to have forgotten yesterday, as each person I met was talking to me as though nothing had occurred yesterday, including Jean, who I am sure is getting fed up with me by the hour. We both wanted to have a look round Stanley Park and its aquarium; this was going to be for starters. I must say it was an excellent place, where first and foremost animal and human safety is paramount.

In the recently completed Beluga Whale Pool, they not only have those creatures, but also dolphins and killer whales. I watched the displays put on by the keepers, including tricks with the whales and dolphins, taking fish from their hands as they jumped across a rock platform, each one named. I did not know this then, but the dorsal fins on the killer whales, male and female, are quite different from each other. Each mammal seemed to be getting great enjoyment from playing games with its minder. There was a substantial guard-rail running round about half of the pool, which the paying public were pressed up against. With huge leaps they would jump out to the water, then with their flippers making an almighty whack, they would create a monstrous splash, and those who had not seen the creatures coming up from the depths would be soaked.

No doubt the chat up line down below was, "Got that lot."

You could walk right down under the pool and around through glass panelling to inspect them at close quarters along with the sea otters, who were in a separate enclosure performing seemingly impossible tricks with their rubber-like bodies.

Jean had decided to take a city bus tour, so I carried on in my own time investigating further this mind-boggling theatre of sea and freshwater fish, etc.

What I did marvel and wonder at were the salmon eggs–hundreds upon hundreds of them in small trays, in various stages of progress, all just about the size of a pinhead and even at this early age, with two very bulbous protruding eyes. I thought them remarkable.

A miniature rain forest was there for us to walk through, with humming birds, brightly coloured parakeets, a magnificent banana tree and there on part of some tree roots lying on the surface were the coils of a giant anaconda. It was visible for several yards so how long it was I would not hazard a guess. The whole place echoed

with the continual chatter of those birds plus the monkeys.
I must have walked a fair distance, as quite abruptly I
thought to myself, enough is enough.

After a quiet late siesta, I washed and changed for the
evening, for I had decided to visit the Dover Arms, an
eating place I had seen earlier in the day when I walked
past. Arriving, I ordered a plate of fish and chips and also
a pint which on arrival looked and tasted like a Guinness.
My remark when the plate arrived was, "Is this all for me
or for two people?"

"No," the young lady replied, "it's all for you."

I duly paid the six and a half dollars (about £4.00
sterling). I must say that it was a splendid pint, again the
froth clinging to the sides like the Irish medicine.

It was about eight-thirty p.m. that a chap came in and
this was when I realised that it was going to be a karaoke
night and there were now quite a number of patrons
coming in. As I was departing the men's room I saw an
elderly couple, and thinking they were English, I asked
them if they were enjoying the trip. Realising that I was,
the man answered, "No, we have been over here for
forty-five years and are now Canadian citizens." They
were both now very interested in me and asked where
was I sitting. I told them, "Right near the DJ."

"Can we come and sit with you on your table?"

"Yes, certainly," was my reply.

We introduced ourselves to each other. Stan was in the
real estate business, and his wife Iris as well, but now
helps only occasionally in the office. I suppose we had
been together for twenty minutes and joining in the songs
being sung when Stan got up and brought back the song-
book saying, "There, Percy, have a go."

I looked all round to see if anyone knew me as I did not want to make a fool of myself, or, rather, the experience. There were a lot of television screens about the place and as the words came up on each one you needn't look in the same direction all the time and you could not forget the words, I marked off "Glasgow Town".

It was a few pints later when Stan said, "It's your turn, Percy! Best of luck." The place, as you can gather, was packed by now and there must have been a lot of Scottish Nationals in there because my voice was almost drowned out by the noise.

Stan and Iris said as I sat down, "Well done," the words hardly out of their mouths when I received a tap on my shoulder. Turning round, a chap with a ruddy complexion says, "You don't say Glasgow Town, you say 'Glasgee Towne'."

"Sorry about that—I'm from England, just outside London."

"Well why don't you sing aboot London Town then? It was na sa bad." Stan had found the book and title.

So I just had to put myself down for that too!

By the time we had had a good chat about the old country it was nearly midnight. In the Dover Arms, it was now time to call it a day and it did not seem as if I would be called upon inside another half hour or so. Thanking them both for their company and wishing them a safe journey home they bade me the same and also a safe passage home.

Outside in the still warm evening air, a night with no clouds, I turned down the street and looked up in the direction of our hotel and there it was, shining out like a Belisha beacon the little "Squiggle"!

The doorman asked, "Had a good evening, sir?"
"Yes I have indeed, goodnight."

Day 12! The day began with Jean and I taking breakfast together. She was catching an earlier flight than ours and her next destination was in the USA, continuing her holiday with relatives.

Back in my room, I completed my packing, and finding that I still had quite a few dollars left decided that after I had taken a walk along the sea front I would use them up.

English Bay is the large expanse of water that runs on the west side of Stanley Park. There is a superb coastal path running along at two levels, one high and the other just up from the shore. I had been told to look for whales here in the bay as quite often they are seen here in October. But, although I kept my beady eye open, no luck–sea otters and plenty of sea birds of many species, no whales.

Margaret, John and Sheila were also out walking and all of us remarked how warm the weather had been, especially today as even the sunbathers were about with a few swimmers for good measure. I had only made their acquaintance on this trip, yet we all seemed to get on with each "like a house on fire" all agreeing how the time had flown so quickly. I told them as I had a few dollars I wanted to get rid of I would see them later.

A few doors down the street from our hotel there was a large shopping precinct and this partly under our hotel: it took you from one street to the other all underground, shops going in all directions.

I spent nearly all my dollars in one shop, the owner being a charming lady with a great sense of humour and ready wit! She wasn't very tall and I would guess not far short of the same measurement going round either. I worked hard to get a discount on each of the items purchased and felt sure that I had made good deals and well on the right side. However, when I worked out my purchases later and how much money I'd spent, I found that I had paid exactly as was marked up on the goods in the first place.

Whilst I was in the shop a tall lad came in; evidently both the owner and he knew one another. So she says to me, "Do you know that you are in the company of a relation of a famous English racing driver?"

I replied, "No, pull the other one!"

Actually, it turned out that he was indeed the cousin of Damon Hill, his uncle being the late Graham Hill. I shook his hand and wished him the best of luck, thanked the lady and left the shop well satisfied.

Back at the hotel after packing away my last purchases, we were all asked to rendezvous in the hotel lobby to present a farewell gift of dollars to Rosa. We all felt she had done us proud, giving everyone a holiday to remember. John gave an excellent speech of appreciation as he presented her with the gift and all our thanks. John did mention my name and from a quick look round the establishment it appeared from their expressions that most of the occurrences I had been involved with had been pardoned and forgotten.

The meeting of the whole company was breaking up, when John came over and said on behalf of Margaret, Sheila and himself, "Will you accept this gift of a wristwatch?" adding, "Now you are in possession of one you should never be late again!"

Thanking him, I said, "I will look after it as long as it appreciates my habits."

All our baggage has now been taken to the coach which is leaving the hotel at one-forty-five p.m. Our flight, though, is not taking off until four-forty-five p.m. All passengers have to be at the airport as is usual throughout the world some two to three hours before take-off time.

While waiting in the departure lounge I recalled some of the events that I had somehow got myself involved with, realising from talking to the other passengers that my being so inquisitive and curious is not the usual "run-of-the-mill stuff" that the group traveller gets entangled with. I did remark to the one or two people who raised this, "I cannot see myself changing at my time of life."

I reminded myself of the Natural History Museum and the totem poles–the totem pole seeds we were given. Who would I give them to on my arrival back home? I did so much want to see the place where they were made and to watch their progress through to their magnificent conclusion.

To go back in time, to have seen those proud Red Indians, how they were able to create an idea, chop the tree down, weave intricate designs, paint it, stand it up, it's mind boggling.

Then there's that proud railway engine that stands in Jasper's rail yard, what a story that would have to tell, reminding me once more of Henry and his noteworthy remarks about those railroaders of the last century when back in 1875 the railway started linking Vancouver on the Pacific to Montreal on the Atlantic side. I should imagine that it must have been correct when he told us that in one day alone (no doubt a decent stretch with no obstacles) six miles and two tons of steel were laid. And this record stands today! What a day that must have been when the railwaymen, those from the east and those from the west, on 7th November 1885, met at a place called Craigellachie.

A brief thought crossed my mind: it most definitely would have had to cross the Fraser Canyon and no doubt many more valleys. That bridge would have had to have been, a timber one, but what a construction to hold that Goliath of steel! Yes, it must have played a huge part in Canada's short history.

Don't get me wrong: Canada has not got a long chronicled history like our own. Yet, millions of years ago, prehistoric animals used to roam this country. For instance there is a place called Drumheller in Alberta where there is an area called "The Dinosaurs' Valley" and there is also a fine museum that houses a collection of fossil and dinosaur remains. I had heard it would have been an interesting visit, but there had been no time to fit this in with our itinerary. A person named L A Duncan had spent a lifetime's work unearthing and listing all his findings, most around the Red Deer River and those studies are still going on today.

The Canadian people with whom I had discussed their country—and there must have been scores—were all of the same makeup, helpful, cheerful, kind and considerate and always with "how to put the world to right" attitudes.

Back now to the present and reality. "CA flight to London Gatwick gate no 8 is boarding" over the Tannoy. Departure time no change, four-forty-five p.m.

I sought out Rosanne and said how sorry I was for my unintentional bad behaviour.

"Percy," she said, "I enjoyed your company and the evening meal we had together at Banff, see you on board."

We had a stopover at Edmonton to pick up more passengers, then next stop London and home. Tuesday, 12th October we arrived just a few minutes past our arrival time of eleven a.m., it had been a comfortable flight and very enjoyable one. I thanked the crew on leaving the aircraft and, quickly through baggage control I said farewell to Margaret, John and Sheila, thanking them for their toleration of me. Spotting Rosanne, we both wished each other the very best for the future, both knowing that in the big world of travel it would be very doubtful if our paths ever crossed again. As she told me in an earlier conversation, each year there are several more countries opening up for tourist trade—so giving her destinations anew, challenges to log up, more miles to add to the thousands already achieved.

Within a few days of arriving home I had left my films for developing. After they had been processed, I was more than pleased with them, especially one, which I think for detail is the best shot I have taken. The occasion was when I and a crowd of different. nationalities were waiting for the large gondola to arrive. at the halfway stage on Grouse Mountain. Directly opposite the terminus was a huge glass panel and the sun was in such a position that all of us were reflected along with the whole of the gondola. Quite a coup! I am sorry that I did not ask all those around me to lift and wave their arms in the air...

I do not profess to be a photographer, not even in the low grade, but I think it is a bit special.

My overall sentiments regarding Canada the Beautiful. It's just that...

West Indies Cricket Tour 1994

I had been waiting for today, Monday 23rd March, for several months now, for I was off to the Caribbean to see the final three test matches with some forty or more England cricket supporters cheering, maybe for some famous England victories.

During this interim period, a number of local cricket enthusiasts had said what a waste of time, as two of the proposed five we had already lost and by big margins. The first one played at Sabina Park, Kingston, Jamaica, we lost by eight wickets, and at the Bourda Ground, Georgetown, Guyana, by an innings and forty-four runs. This, though, made not the slightest difference, for I was determined to provide another voice of encouragement.

The taxi arrived right on the dot at five-thirty a.m. to get me to Chingford Station to catch the five-fifty-five train to Liverpool Street, a change from rail to underground at Walthamstow Central, through to Victoria, thence the Gatwick Express, arriving at the airport at seven-ten a.m. in plenty of time for my flight at nine-fifteen.

I considered everything to be going according to plan so far—up to the entrance hall, and as I could not see any signs up for Terminal 4, I enquired of a couple of red-coated Virgin stewardesses if they could point me in the direction of Terminal 4.

"You are at the wrong airport," one quickly replied.

"I can't be," I argued, diving into my hand luggage bag for my travel documents, finding them. "Have a look at them." Then a quick check from all the receptionists, now three with the same answer simultaneously, "WIAA Terminal 4, Heathrow."

I don't mind telling you I was in a state of shock, and now finding my spectacles, I could see for myself that indeed I was at the wrong airport. Another Virgin stewardess had now arrived and asked, "What company are you travelling with, sir?"

I just could not come to terms with the realisation of how promptly the brakes had been applied to my progress by my being at the wrong airport.

"The Mike Burton Group," I answered in an aggrieved voice.

"What time is your flight, sir?"

"Nine-fifteen," I meekly replied to this further enquiry.

It appeared that this was the senior stewardess, who was now taking control of the situation, and giving me lots of reassurance saying, "What we will do is try to get you on the shuttle bus which calls here at seven-thirty to pick up passengers to Heathrow. Follow me."

At the coach departure lounge some fifteen people were waiting! The Virgin stewardess explained my problem to the receptionist, who in turn replied in a loud voice, "The bus is running late, about five minutes, and there are only five seats available on it, and they go to the first ticket-holders."

The Virgin stewardess said to me, "Sit down and we will see what turns up."

"Is there any other way I can get to Heathrow?" I asked.

"Only by taxi, and that will cost you a bomb," she replied.

Then a voice came from an elderly lady sitting in a corner. "I am not in a hurry, shall we exchange tickets?"

I thanked her most kindly, accepting this offer. While this exchange went ahead, another stewardess had arrived who told me she was going to Heathrow and would see me through to check-in. I thanked her companion for all the help she had given me and she wished me luck. Only a few more minutes and the shuttle bus pulled in, my seat at the rear the last one available.

The stewardess I was travelling with was seated just a couple of seats in front, and said to me, "Let's hope you make your flight."

And the time now just after leaving?–looking at the clock to the left of the driver's head, seven-thirty-two.

"About forty minutes' drive," the person said to me in the next seat. At this stage I clearly remember thinking, plenty of time to book in and buy some duty frees, and a cuppa before departure!

The signposted mileage rapidly improved in my favour and when we reached one that indicated six miles to Heathrow, and the clock showed eight-fifteen, I thought, "Should be time to meet some of my fellow travellers." Then the traffic started building and building; there was hardly any progress at all, hundreds of vehicles all round us. I could clearly see the airport, unfortunately for every minute's forward movement, there would be five stationary ones. The Virgin stewardess had looked round several times, giving little nods of encouragement. But at 9.20, just after an ear-shattering roar of engines she turned round to me, smiled and mouthed upward to the sky with her finger: "That's your flight taking off."

At this instant, all sorts of things went through my mind, the most prominent thought being, "What an idiot to go to the wrong airport in the first place!"

Getting off the coach, she guided me through to where I should have been two hours ago, the Canadian Airways desk where they were dealing with the WIAA passengers. I thanked her for helping me to get this far.

As soon as I made myself known as to who I was, there was an immediate cry of, "The one that got away has arrived," from the girl at check-in. I must say straightaway, I don't believe any passenger could have received better treatment than those Canadian Airways stewardesses gave me. I was treated like royalty, as I am sure my anxiety was beginning to surface. The one in charge told me they had already been in touch with the Mike Burton office by fax as early as seven-fifteen, telling them that I had gone to Gatwick instead of Heathrow. She informed me that the next direct flight to Port of Spain was not until tomorrow. "Not to worry, sir; we are trying to re-route you through another country. Pop and have a cuppa and you'll feel better in no time."

Ten minutes later she called over to me, "Your baggage, sir. We have booked you on a flight to Miami with American Airways. Here are your tickets, right through to

Port of Spain. Flight times are also there for your connection. You should arrive at Port of Spain at approximately nine-thirty p.m. Have a good flight."

I could not thank the Canadian Airways stewardesses enough, shaking each girl's hand, each wishing me well, and hoping the England Team would succeed and bring back the Ashes.

My flight to Miami International was very comfortable. At one stage I had a brief conversation with another passenger also sitting in an aisle seat. He said to me, starting the exchange, "I noticed your hand-luggage address; you don't live very far from where I live."

I said, "Oh, where is that?"

"Waltham Abbey. I am taking my family to Disney Land for a short break. And where are you going to?" he asked.

When I told him where I was heading, the West Indies, and how I came to be aboard this aeroplane, he replied, "I must say, I have never heard of that before, going to the wrong airport. Are you going there for a holiday?"

My reply: "No, I was going to support the England Cricket Team."

He laughed at this, saying, "I play a bit of cricket myself." We talked about cricket for a short time, concluding our conversation when he told me his name was De Silva. As soon as he said that I knew the team he played for and knew also of the useful batting scores he had put together, including those against my own village team, High Beech. Enough had been said, and tactfully changing the subject, we talked of other things.

Miami International

It seemed when we alighted from the aircraft that, wherever you looked, police were everywhere, and all carrying arms. I still had not purchased any films for my camera, as I had not had any time to search out the duty-frees at Heathrow, so I went through the passport, immigration, and visa barriers. Having a quick look round, I saw no sign of any shops, so I decided to turn round and go back, get a cuppa and go to Departures.

This was going to be more difficult that I had dared to imagine. Not only had I got to go back the way I had come, but also through luggage and personal barriers, so that afterwards I was sorry that I had wanted to leave the Departure Lounge in the first place.

My baggage went through the screen, and, moving round to retrieve it, a large hand wrapped itself round mine, and another hand was soon holding my shoulder in a vice-like grip. I could not have moved a muscle even if I had wanted to.

Turning my head and seeing three huge policemen, with their hands on the artillery hanging from the holsters slung from their waist belts, I said, "Hold on, officers, what's up?"

"Not so fast," said the one, easing the grip on my wrist and shoulder, "Now what have you got in that bag?"

I don't mind telling you that all sorts of instances flash through your mind in situations like this. Well, they do for me! And the first thing that flashed across my mind was drugs. Had anyone planted any drugs on me? That passenger Da Silva! What had be been up to, especially when he noticed the address on this very same bag?

"Nothing," I said, "only a few things I might need to get to quickly."

"Our screen does not tell lies; we are going to search your bag, and confiscate the fruit you have in there," a police sergeant said.

"Fruit, fruit, yes of course I have some fruit in there. I have three plums, the remaining ones from the pound I purchased last Saturday at Sainsbury's. Is that all?"

Putting my hand in the bag, bringing them out into daylight, they were indeed a sorry sight, for only one was pleasant to the eye, the other two looked as if they had been sat on. In any case the sergeant took them, and giving the rest of the contents a thorough examination. I told him, "I am only sorry that I did not eat them on the way over. I would have done if I had known I was going to cause all this trouble."

The policeman who had held my shoulder and wrist now returned with a large board, placed it in front of me and said, "Read that, buddy."

Briefly, it said that it was illegal to bring into the country any fruit, et cetera, of any description, together with plants, et cetera, or take anything out.

I said how sorry I was for not reading those regulations before. Was I glad to be free from them, and also the twenty or so people who had gathered round to witness and presumably see what action might transpire from the "Old Fella"!

Our flight left at four-forty-five for Port of Spain. Looking down on Miami International, I breathed a sigh of relief, vowing that it was going to be a long time, if ever, before I returned to this airport. Our flight path took us over parts of, on one side the Atlantic Ocean, and on the other, the Caribbean Sea. The pilot kept us well informed of all the various places of interest we were passing over, and as darkness fell, told us to look for the lights of different islands as we flew over. Without exaggeration, I am sure we saw scores of them.

Just before eight-forty-five he said, "Fasten your seat belts, we are landing approximately fifteen minutes late." I do know something, this was going to be only the second time in my life that I was arriving in a foreign country, in my own company, and having to make decisions for myself. The first thing to do was retrieve my suitcase from the conveyor belt. This was going to take longer than I thought, for all around me, everybody was talking a strange language. Now and again I picked up the words, then all of a sudden very fast arguments would break out, and in this pigeon English! I defy anyone to understand what a conversation is all about if only three people are involved, and here there were scores like this all going on at the same time.

By the time I had located my suitcase, and the noise from these individuals was now at times deafening, I was feeling a little concerned, as I was wondering how fate was going to work for me this time. I had eased my way through to where a line of islanders were holding boards above their heads. One said, "Sammon". I thought it had to be me although it was misspelt. I walked over to the chap holding it and told him who I was.

"You with Mr Mike Burton?" he asked.

"Yes," I replied.

"Mr Kelly has sent me to pick you up and take you to the Upside Down Hotel," he said as he picked up my suitcase, walking towards his taxi. Upside Down Hotel I thought! Where's that? "I'm supposed to be going to the Hilton Hotel," I answered anxiously.

"Yes, you are, sir, but we taxi drivers call it the Upside Down Hotel because more floors are down than up. For the life of me, I could not fathom this remark.

My case safely in the boot, I was then subjected to a pretty rough ride through the pitch dark—very little street lighting, and as for headlights? The road we were travelling over seemed more like a motorcycle-scramble course than a public highway—they weren't little potholes! At times, you seemed to be riding in them! I mentioned this accumulation of hazards to Alfred (who was going to be a very jovial warm-hearted avid West Indian cricket supporter in days to come).

He had now made himself known to me: "You must call me Alfred."

I don't think Alfred stopped talking all the rest of the way to the hotel.

"Our government is spending a lot of money improving all the roads on the island, and next year it is hoped sufficient funds will be available to resurface the whole of the road to the airport.

After some twenty minutes, we started climbing round some easy S-bends on this quite sharp gradient, and Alfred came at last to a halt, saying, "The Upside Down Hotel, Mr Salmon."

Looking at the Hilton in the darkness, I still could not see why the taxi drivers called it by this name. I thanked Alfred who said, "I don't know why you have come all this way to see your team beaten, man!"

One thing I did know for certain, I never dreamed at nine this morning that I would see this place, then I realised that as there is a four-hour time difference it was now ten-ten p.m., so back in England it was already tomorrow.

I went straight to the reception, and told one of the three receptionists I was expected, but was a bit late. No sooner had I told her I was with the Mike Burton Group of English cricket supporters, than a hand was placed on my shoulder and I turned round to see a jovial-looking man holding out his hand saying, "You must be Percy, I am Terry Kelly from Yorkshire."

From that first meeting, Telly Kelly was how I always referred to him, face or otherwise. He struck me straightaway as a caring and conscientious person, and I suppose, being a tour manager, he had to have this positive attitude about him.

I completed my business with the concierge, feeling a bit shell-shocked from parting with so much money without any reward. She had asked me for a deposit of a traveller's cheque. This payment was for any meals, drinks, whatever, etc. and for finally squaring my account on leaving the hotel. £200 was a lot of money.

Telly Kelly could see that I was concerned parting with this small fortune and said, "Don't worry, Percy, everybody has choices: pay a deposit now, then receive the difference when we leave, or pay up straightaway. Come over here and meet John and Liz."

They told me that they did not leave Heathrow until ten-thirty a.m. and had only been in the hotel just over an hour. They both made me feel welcome; in fact, Liz welcomed me like a long-lost cousin. How, what, why, when, umpteen questions. I told them the whole story and assured them that I was all right after my experience in

Miami, and that I had learnt my lesson concerning smuggled fruit.

I had a couple of glasses with them and then told them I was going to bed, the time now eleven-thirty. Telly Kelly says, "You know you have got to go down to the twelfth floor, see you in the morning."

I think it was only on this occasion for the first time that the penny dropped, and indeed the Upside Down Hotel was really was built that way, so instead of going up to the twelfth I was going down. It must be similar to the one that I was in, during my stay in Canada. What a room, two king-sized beds! The nearest one I flopped out on and am sure went straight to sleep.

Day 2

Drawing my curtains in the morning, I realised this hotel had been built in a primary position, for looking down from my veranda I could see another two floors, almost within touching distance. There were a dozen or so bamboo trees, at least thirty feet high, with nice thoughtfully planned garden planting. Lush was the operative word. A pathway led down to three tennis courts, all enclosed with a twelve-foot high security fence. I would estimate all this was at least forty feet below where I was standing. I was here for another nine nights; what a place!

I started to investigate the room, finding that the television had a built-in clock, so I was not going to have any problems about a timepiece. Given the size of the bathroom, wardrobe, et cetera, this room could cater for a family of six without any difficulty.

Next–up to the breakfast room. Soon ready for a new day, I walked up to the area, which contained the notice boards. I was reading the Mike Burton notice for events arranged for today, when out of the corner of my eye I spotted Tom Graveney sitting reading a newspaper. (Tom was with the Mike Burton outfit as our celebrity person.) So I went across and introduced myself.

Shaking my hand he said, "You know, Percy, I have been longing to meet you, you realise you are a first as far as I am concerned, to go to the wrong airport to leave the Old Country."

He was just the sort of person I imagined from that first introduction, his careful selection of words making you feel sure that your company to him was just as important as his was going to be to you. Any time I was in his company I felt completely at ease, which made me feel a bit special. Of course, cricket was the main subject when you were talking and, as now, you felt you had to ask him his thoughts on the Test Series so far, and the matches to come.

I don't want to dwell on his contribution to his country in days gone by with the willow. His record speaks for itself, whatever continent he has played in, his offering was one hundred per cent.

Then he asked me what I had planned for today, as the Test didn't start until tomorrow. I am glad cricket and my airport misbehaviour were now behind me for a time, so I said, "I saw on the notice board that there is an excursion to the ASA Wright Nature Reserve."

"If you like nature in its truest sense, then you'll enjoy it up there," Tom said. "Have a good day."

There was quite a bit of time left before the coach departed, so I decided to walk down the pathway to the busy highway that I could see from my bedroom window.

Reaching the bottom, I crossed the road and reached a large expanse of greenery which, now I was close to, looked a hell of a lot more extensive than at first impression.

An old gentleman was sitting on one of the wooden seats, presumably after some jogging. I asked if I could sit down beside him for a while. Very soon, he was telling me all about this roundabout, for indeed that is what it was. It's supposed to be the largest in the world, approximately two and a half miles round and it is called a Savannah. He had just jogged round its entire length.

I felt a bit mean when I said to him, "Do you only do the one circuit?" and surprised when he said, "No, sometimes I do two and a half laps—that's if I feel like it."

I continued, "I'll see you tomorrow," and off I walked back up the hill to the hotel. I would say it was a good half-mile and on the way back I noticed on the hotel side of the pathway a termite track with hundreds going up and coming down. Their own pathway was on the topside of an open rainfall gully running parallel with the pedestrian pathway. This concrete open culvert was four feet wide by five feet high and perched on top were one-metre lengths of granite kerbing one and a half inches wide, and this was where the comings and goings were being negotiated.

I though at the first opportunity I would find out what those one-inch long Goliaths had found so attractive, for turning round and looking back down the hill, what a distance! And each one on the journey back up was carrying something.

There were five of us on the coach, a type of Bedford truck with sliding doors to get in and out. There were two couples, one of these being the England cricket-scorer Alec Davis and his good lady. I could not believe my luck, for here I was only a few hours into my holiday and already I had met Tom Graveney and, of all people, one of the most important men associated with cricket. His records through the years will be carefully scrutinised, much as will be his own account that he was logging—and a Warwickshire County scorer to boot. Whew! And then while talking to him on the way up, I discover that in our hotel are the entire West Indian Team, all the England Team plus the BBC and their complement, and also sports reporters.

The ASA Wright Nature Reserve is about six miles up and off the main highway. A series of S-bends took us there on the Blanchisseuse road. This was a bit special, for as we climbed higher and higher on this one-track road, cocoa trees, citrus, coffee and banana plantations were all round us and below in the Aripo Valley. Our driver informed us that this was also rain forest that we were passing through. We all agreed it was a good job the weather prospects were in our favour.

The clearing and entrance to the Reserve came very unexpectedly. This was where the forest had been cut away, and the whole area had been turned into a nature reserve. We had to wait for our guide to come to conduct us round. While we awaited his arrival I noticed that part of the building we were standing in had quite a substantial veranda. Everywhere you looked all was made of wood: this area, twenty feet long by six feet wide, had a nice sensible balustrade, approximately three feet high, running the entire length. Hanging from the substantial beams were bird tables set at regular intervals, with each one attended by humming birds of all sizes and colours that defy the imagination. They were fantastic! If I said there were as many as ten to twenty birds at one time along this stretch, I would not be telling porkies.

This building overlooked the Aripo Rain Forest below us, and as we gazed down on the unstirring tree tops, this stillness and tranquillity was being broken only by the chatter of the birds around us. Of course, the snappers were here as well as the Mike Burton contingent, all trying to capture on film, perhaps a humming bird two feet away from the lens! All I have to show for my efforts at a later date, are several photos with blurs, but a superb background! I don't believe I have ever been so close to the like before, and it was an occasion when I wished I had, like some of the others, a camera with a telescopic lens. A bird I studied, about eighteen inches away, was hovering at eye level, the bird itself perhaps four inches in length. Its colouring was breathtaking and, of course, I could not pick up the wing beats, though, remarkably, in a nearby room excellent photos were on display complete with the whole bird outline, performing over the very same tables. I wonder how many thought like me at the time, do they ever collide?

Thomas, a Trinidadian, had now arrived, collecting us all together, some twenty-five people of all nationalities. We then embarked on a very enlightening one and a half hours of nature trail – trees, birds, butterflies, insects, you name it, and if it was anywhere near where we walked through, I'm sure we saw it.

I must say Thomas was only a young lad, but certainly knew his stuff. Often he would tell us the Latin name of a particular subject, then he would ask if any of us would like to correct his pronunciation of that species or specimen. There was, I suspect, one professional person, who was carrying a huge case of camera equipment. Now and again he would bring out a very expensive camera, fix up the tripod and telescopic lens, take a snap and just as quickly dismantle and return everything back to the case and then make a note in his fair-sized (I have not the slightest doubt.) Latin phrase book!

We had been walking for about half an hour when we came to a dried-up stream. Crossing over it by a narrow bridge, Thomas then decided to give us all some knowledge of the insect world, their habits and a general chat about their lifestyle and how they play a major part in the upkeep of the rain forest.

"Now I don't mind telling you, we have some enormous tarantulas here in Trinidad, and in this part of the forest we have some with six inches of body, not including the eight legs, so you can gather they are pretty huge" – placing his hands together – "about this size."

"Whew!" we all gasped.

Supporting the bridge some of us were standing on, were four stout posts in each corner. One young lady was leaning against one of those, just another very interested listener, like the rest of us. Of course, most of us were on the alert straightaway, looking up the trees to spot something of this size moving through the branches.

Thomas quite calmly walked across to the young lady and said, "Do you know you are sitting on one?" gently taking her arm and leading her away from what we all thought to be imminent danger. I was standing quite near and noticed the post-top was hollow and had an aperture of four to six inches.

The young lady? I can't recall a person's face change

colour so dramatically. Within a second of Thomas removing her from the danger zone, and now, as we all looked at her, what was a nice glowing healthy complexion was now a shade of white very difficult to describe.

Thomas, realising that this had affected the young lady quite badly said, "Don't worry, you will come to no harm. In the day-time, it is usually asleep, especially in this hot weather. Now if you all look closely you will see for yourselves the funnel-shaped web he comes up through, to sit on the top of the post waiting for meals to come along."

By now the young lady was regaining her colour, and was none the worse for her experience of sitting on a tarantula.

Moving on it did not matter where we stopped, Thomas always seemed to make an area special. There were termite trails leading to gigantic nests, (I thought of the one near the hotel, surely not a nest of those proportions?), bamboo trees we could not see the top of, the forest being so dense, and then, one for our photographer friend, a butterfly orchid. Thomas says it is quite rare, it was about twelve feet up from the ground and hidden behind some foliage. Thomas said if we moved up onto the higher ground we would see it in full bloom. This we all succeeded in doing and the snapper was over the moon, letting his guard down when he described it in a luxuriant Latin name.

Returning to base, there was time now to explore the rest of the building as our lunch was not quite prepared. Some fifty or more stuffed birds common to the island were on display in another part of the building we had looked at earlier and also more photos, this time of the flora and fauna of the island. I am not sure if anyone saw an iguana inside, but certainly there were plenty outside, their colouring remarkable, I had spotted one through the open window, and the other couple who formed our party asked what it was that had taken my interest. I told them to look carefully at a certain piece of limestone rock that had two of them sitting on it, but neither could see them and the more I looked at them the more their camouflaged bodies became very difficult to spot, especially as the sun had reached them so it appeared as if the whole was one.

"Lunch is served," came the shout from inside the restaurant—a rack of beef, vegetables and potatoes washed down with either Caribs, or red or white wine.

Three-quarters of an hour later our journey back to civilisation started. This was an even more compelling drive than the one we made coming up. The S-bends we negotiated seemed to arrive just as uphill traffic was also in the immediate forested vicinity. As the Aripo Valley was on our right side the driver worked miracles to keep the bus on the highway, and avoid the big drop, which was my view for a good quarter of an hour.

What was even more disturbing was when the potholes arrived. They shook my nerves to the limits, for they were right on the part of road which had been given severe treatment by vehicles, and as I gazed out of this near-side window to the area below, all I could see for protection were the few concrete posts with a tubed piece of metal, acting as a guard rail Since this sadly looked the worse for wear I prayed quietly to myself for our safety.

Back at the hotel, everyone I had been with during the day had enjoyed the trip, and with a "see you tomorrow" the last remark between us, I went down, had a wash and brush up, a change, an evening meal and a couple of Caribs, and I was soon in bed, time ten-thirty p.m.

Day 3 - Day 1 Third Test Match

Going up to breakfast and joining the queue, I found myself standing next to Keith Fletcher, the England manager, I shook his hand and wished him the best of luck as looking round the dining room I noticed several cricketers of both countries having their breakfast.

A coach came to pick us up at nine a.m., dropping us off in the vicinity of the Queen's Park Oval. Soon in the ground and walking along talking to Tom Graveney, when coming towards us was Sir Gary Sobers. Of course, they knew each other instantly. "Hello, Tom." "Hello, Gary, this is my friend Percy who is visiting the West Indies for the first time."

I shook the great man's hand, there were a few "good lucks" all round, then we walked on. I thanked Tom very much for the introduction and he replied, "You know, Percy, Gary is a super person on and off the field. With him there are no airs and graces, he's a natural." For a while I walked round in a bit of a daze, thinking how Tom had made me feel so comfortable, talking to cricketers in the top league. I decided to go for a few Caribs.

I want to make it perfectly clear, as now I am now about to involve the reader in quite a number of pages, about how my trip to watch the West Indies Cricket Tour came about. I have a reasonable knowledge of cricket, most of my activity, if not all, in connection with local friendly games, with the occasional Derby games with neighbouring villages. With regard to county cricket, players and their performances, who scored the most runs, who took the most wickets. I could not even tell you how my own county, Essex, has fared through the years. I know they have won several championships, and a few trophies, but the years? Sorry. Through the years—that's probably forty-five—I daresay I would have averaged one game a season, that's watching the county's competitive matches.

Now you might be saying after reading the last paragraphs, "What's he doing there?" Well, we all promise ourselves, "If only I had the opportunity to do so-and-so..." One of mine has always been to see a test match abroad and no, I have never seen one in England either, and here I am, and I've just been in the company of two of the greatest test cricketers to have graced the game.

So here we are at this test venue at the Oval, Port of Spain. What instantly struck me were the huge trees dotted around the grounds with limbs and branches, of almost equal girth as the main trunk. I was over the moon when I was informed that the tree is called a *saman*, when I asked the name of those gigantic masterpieces. I remembered that Alfred, the taxi cab driver, had spelt my name similarly on his notice board at the airport. I only wish I could have been built the same way! The next few days during most of the breaks I was glad to sit underneath the big one behind our stand—and, my! did it get some abuse, from West Indian supporters, using it for all sorts of purposes. The leaves are very similar to our laburnum at home, but almost threadlike in comparison. Near this specimen, there was a Trinidadian with a huge machete topping and tailing coconuts, then selling them at five dollars each. Most of the time he had a good trade going, beside the Carib beer there was also a Red Strike, very similar in taste, but just the label the difference. I found both drinkable, and I, like a good many more England supporters, put quite a few away during the course of the day.

The West Indies had won the toss, and had decided to bat, and as most of the learned supporters I was sitting with were saying, this was a surprise, for their front-line bowlers Curtly Ambrose and Courtney Walsh were fit and ready for action.

At the close of play, they were 227 for 7 wickets. Angus Fraser our medium-paced bowler had bowled well for us, his figures at the end of play were 21, 9, 37, 2 and if two catches had been held, who knows, the West Indies might have been fielding.

On the coach back, everybody seemed to be in a confident mood.

In the evening, the hotel put on a barbecue beside the swimming pool. It seemed that anyone who was important to both the West Indies and England were there—cricketers who had now retired, most indulging in a tipple or two or three. Most of the conversation was about how well England had contained the big guns of the West Indies from getting on top, with Angus Fraser at the forefront of the chatter...

I had a good wander round talking to various celebrities. I found it was quite easy to get them to tell me their thoughts on the way this Third Test had started, and their opinions.

Day 4 - 2nd day of Third Test Match

I was up at six a.m., deciding that I would walk the short distance round the Savannah. On the inside of the highway, approximately twenty feet apart, was a line of various species of trees that followed the curvature of the road. Some of these were packed with red, pink or white blossoms; none of the trees varied in height, all were about fifteen metres high. I was later in the day to find out they are *terbuia*.

In the dining room I saw a chap sitting by himself and asked if I could join him. We introduced ourselves. Keith Booth was over here doing the scoring for BBC Television. I felt highly honoured to be in his company and told him so. I told him that I had been in the company of Alec Davis, the Warwickshire County scorer, who is over here scoring for England. I also told him about my banner that the cricket club ladies had made up for me to hang up so when the camera picked it up they would know that I was there. "Where do you think I should place it for the best position?" I asked Keith.

"If you put it anywhere along the front of the Jeff Stolmeyer stand, any of the cameras will pick it up." He tells me he is writing a book all about the test series.

I said, "I should think it will be very interesting." We then got round to the present situation, and how many more runs can the West Indies put on for the last three wickets.

I had purchased some rolls, butter and cheese, making them up into three packs and placing them in a carrier bag before I boarded the coach, so I was ready for the day's action.

The West Indies only added another twenty-five runs before they were all out for 252. Angus Frazer returned figures of 29, 9, 49, 4. Chris Lewis, with 25, 2, 61, 4, gave him excellent support. At the end of the day's play,

England was 236 for 6 wickets. Graham Thorpe was 64 not out, and everybody on the coach back was in a jovial mood.

Directly opposite on the other side of the ground where we had our seats during the day, a West Indian band, with the drummer making sure everybody in the ground heard him, was a continuing attraction all day long. What I found hard work was the going up and down the concrete steps to the bars for drinks, and the like. One thing was a bonus–the food I had prepared saved a lot of queuing.

Everyone in the group were good company, and when I told them I had brought and put up a banner, most nearby seat occupants would say, "I bet folks back home saw that," when a ball was hit towards the area where I had tied it up.

Telly Kelly is just as my first impression was, a very conscientious tour manager. There is an elderly lady with us on her own, Mrs Spicer, who comes from Somerset and is a county member and at our first meeting and introduction she said to me, "You know, Percy, both our counties, Essex and Somerset, have always got on well together, and I trust we continue to do so." Telly Kelly was seldom very far away from Enid, sitting nearby and keeping a watchful eye open, and at times looking quite concerned if his charge disappeared from view.

It had again been very warm during the day, and back in the hotel a very different temperature, with the air-cooling system working magnificently, wash and change, an evening meal, a few Caribs and bed.

Day 5 - 3rd day of Third Test Match

An early morning stroll down to and partway round the Savannah, spotting Keith Booth turning his arm over on what looked like the only decent piece of ground for bowling on as you cast your eye round the waste land around him—only slow bowling by the look of the action.

Back at breakfast, this soon completed, I had already purchased my sustenance for the day. On the coach and sitting near to Enid, I asked her, "Do you have a little nod during the game?!"

"Percy! Nodding off, not likely, you don't think I have come all this way from Somerset to go to sleep, do you?"

"Well, I only asked," and looking at her I could see she was not amused.

Arriving at the ground, I had quickly cottoned on that you have to be at the forefront of those England supporters who wanted to put their banners up, the reason being that the first in the ground could move in and select the best position for the TV cameras. Thus I ensured myself a good chance that the banner would be spotted at home. This morning I moved it round to a different place from yesterday, hanging on the perimeter fence with, on the other side, a rum seller and a kiosk. I asked them if they would keep an eye on it for me during the day, so of course I had to purchase a rum and coke now and then. It turned out to be a much hotter day, in fact very humid, and at times stifling. I was glad when the breaks came. At the lunch break I moved to sit near the saman tree, eating my rolls, washing them down with a couple of Caribs, all the time watching the coconut man pick up a coconut, then with the point of his machete stab a hole in it, and prepare it for a customer. Magic!

At the close of play England were all out for 328, and in reply in their second knock, West Indies had lost 5 wickets in scoring 143. On our coach back the Supporters were in jubilant mood, the West Indies only 67 runs on and 5 of their best batsmen back in the pavilion, England now in a fine position and well on top. As there is a rest day tomorrow, Monday, the match would then restart again on Tuesday, so the green ones among us, and I have no doubt I would be a leading contender, we thought, all will be over by nightfall this coming Tuesday in our favour. The odd one or two were saying, "Remember we have got to bat last on that track," or "They will make it difficult whatever target the West Indies set us." I did overhear one person say, "It's only rain that will save them now."

Back at the hotel and reading the notice board for tomorrow's excursions–a trip to Tobago by plane. It was going to cost 630 dollars or about £80, with a barby as well, so I put my name down.

Day 6

We left the hotel at seven-thirty a.m., some twenty supporters. Our flight left at ten, only taking twenty minutes; thankfully the weather was blue skies and the promise of this all day. A coach took us to a place called Pigeon Point, where quite a number went into the sea for a dip, while the rest of us admired the swaying palm trees loaded with their monster fruit; some of the coconuts were lying round the base of the trunks. William, one of the guides, tells us that if you were underneath and one hit you, you would receive a nasty headache. I'm sure he was right and, seeing them closely, I would say a direct hit could split your skull open.

At eleven-thirty a glass-bottomed boat arrives to take us all out to the coral reefs some eleven and a half miles out. You could see the area we were aiming for by the breakers smashing into them, and, sure thing, on arrival the rocks were either just under or just below the surface. Looking through the glass bottom, I felt mesmerised by it all. I cannot recall ever imagining sea water so clear; the depth of this William tells us is about four feet. We had all been invited to borrow sandals and snorkelling equipment, and investigate the mysteries of this underwater paradise. Most went in to examine the coral that was now becoming more and more vivid in colour, and umpteen sea creatures.

I sat there overwhelmed by the beauty of it all. The engines had long been shut down and now the boat was just allowing the gentle swell to let us drift along. William was telling the five of us left on board what sort of coral we should be looking for and what it looked like. As soon as he mentioned one, there it was in all its glory, a brain coral.

Just a couple of feet below me, it was as if I was looking at an identical workings of a human brain, grey in colour with everything you associate with a brain. Of course, now we had seen one, we spotted more and more of them but nothing like the size of the first discovery. We then came to an area where a lot of fish had collected, with colours that defy the imagination. We had a chap with a camera and telescopic lens; he was going bananas.

Starting up again, with everyone back on board, we

stopped again where the coral was not quite so plentiful. It was the seabed this time. William tells us that it is known as the Nylon Beach, for, as you looked through the glass, it looked so white that it seemed as if the white Tide man had paid a visit.

I could not resist it any longer. I decided to go in and enjoy the luxury that all the others were deriving pleasure from. William had said, "It's just a metre deep," so I fixed myself up with sandals and snorkel, walked down the side of the boat and dropped in. I can honestly say as I read from my diary that it is accurate. It says, "The sand is just like walking on silk." I was soon like the rest of the swimmers, searching and feeling the texture of this miracle sand. As your feet went into the sand, they seemed to be moving through a field of cut-up silken thread. I know I said at the time, "I don't expect to witness anything like this again." Certainly, the goggles played a big part in enjoying the close-ups of what was around you, the friendliness of the tropical fish so abundant all around us all. As I gazed at them in awe I considered how my ancestors, and those of the fish too, had seen dramatic changes in sea transport that had come to investigate them, through history.

After twenty minutes, both the guides called to us to come back on board. Now was going to be the difficult part; it was all right dropping in the water, but it was getting out that I had not considered (for I was unable to bend my leg). The step I was trying to reach was about one foot up from the surface of the water. Whatever I tried to do to pull myself up, it refused to bend. "Try the other leg first," came the cry from all round the boat, including Telly Kelly and John and Liz sunbathing on top of the boat's cabin. Both guides could see that I was not going to get back without help. "Leave him there," came the shout this time. The other guide had now grabbed my arms and was trying to pull me on board. Then William cut the engines, dropped in the sea, grabbed both my legs, and shoved me back into the boat with the other chap nearly pulling my arms from their sockets. This was all done to great applause and clapping from everyone on the boat.

Back at the beach the barby was now ready with kingfish, snapper, chicken, baked spuds, all washed down with wine, beer and spirits (rum). I must say straightaway, most everyone was a stranger to each other, and it's quite amazing how a do like this can soon melt the ice. By the time the coach arrived to take us for a trip round the island, most were on first-name terms with everyone in the party.

Quite a number, noticing that the rum was of a special variety, soon consumed it, and very little liquid refreshment was left when the coach arrived to pick us up. For about two hours of the excursion we were taken to lots of Tobago's tourist spots—our first stop Scarborough an old fort of days of the SAIL, complete with cannons of the period. Then we were travelling along the west coast to Plymouth—coconut plantations, the road winding and undulating. This surface we could not grumble about—only the odd pothole, but who worried about them? There were palm trees on one side of the coach, the sea on the other. The spectacular colouring of the sea at times took your breath away, so vivid a blue that I would defy any artist to paint this true colour scheme, and round the next corner, another expanse of water of a different shade. We passed through the Mount Irvine Resort, with waving palm trees on each side of the road. Of course, this was a golf course with all its manicured greens and fairways. The driver stopped, and all eyes from the near-side window watched the couple approaching. The woman was a real black stunner, and her companion did not need much recognising–a straw-boatered Geoffrey Boycott, no less. Nobody said a word until he laid into his drive from the tee. We all saw the ball fly into some scrub on the right-hand side of the fairway, so this seemed a good time to give him some sledging. Lots of remarks were made to Geoffrey, but the most appropriate one, the lad from Wales, Ian shouted out a bit louder than the rest of us, "You have got to get on the front foot, Geoffrey." A big cheer from the coach! Turning and waving, he did not say a word, just gave us his big grin. His girlfriend seemed totally unaware of the noisy England cricket supporters.

This was a conversation piece for some time, wondering who was his companion.

Back to the airport, all the connection times linked up very efficiently. At eight-forty-five I had an evening meal with Enid, a few drinks with the lads, happy to recap an eventful day, and how everything had gone according to plan.

Day 7 - 4th day of 3rd Test Match

I was up nice and early to go for my customary walk round the Savannah, so after my good half-hour's activity I looked forward to breakfast, and a chat with Alfred and his taxi pals. As usual the banter was, "You are not going to watch your team? What a waste of time!"

"You wait and see," was my reply.

All were in jubilant mood again at breakfast as well as on the coach, quite sure a result was going to be in our favour, by as early as mid-afternoon. There were two or three people thinking on these lines, myself included.

The West Indies continued to bat, but not score in their usual cavalier fashion, yet still adding useful runs, then about noon the heavens opened and sheets of rain kept crossing over the ground. We were well sheltered from all of this, I had made one attempt to go and retrieve my banner, but when most of my companions said leave it there, that is what I decided. Play started again when an area of blue appeared, so the Test Panel decided that nineteen overs were lost, and if possible extra overs would be played later on, weather permitting.

Of course the West Indian supporters were loving this big climatic change, and now there was incessant drum beating, banging, shouting, cheering, in fact a racket the like I confess I never witnessed before, well not at a cricket match: West Indies 269 all out.

England now needed to score 194 to win, with 15 overs left to bowl today, and all tomorrow to get them in. One of the lads with us, a betting chap, had told us that he had taken odds-on for England to win the match.

The weather now had changed again to cloudy and humid conditions, to help the West Indian bowlers. One after the other, our wickets started to fall. Curtly Ambrose, we all agreed, was unplayable, his figures of 6 for 22 from one ball short of 8 overs said it all. Close of play—40 for 8 wickets.

Not only were all our lads shell-shocked and demoralised, but all us supporters were as well. We just could not believe it had happened so quickly, and it had all come in such a short time. We all breathed a sigh of relief when stumps were drawn. As for my poor banner: most of the colours had all run–reds, blues, yellows and blacks all now mixed like the hues and tints of a rainbow.

Even the rum-sellers were stunned because very few English supporters were propping up the bar. On the coach back to the hotel, very few showed any sign of wanting to come along to see the finish tomorrow. If I said straightaway that it seemed that we were in a funeral cortège, you would get the mood of our contingent. One chap who has quite a decent pair of binoculars remarked, "The ball was moving about so much, I just could not pick up the flight." I admit I never saw anything–only the stumps being knocked down, or hand-clapping amongst the West Indies fielders.

Each and every one played as if they were possessed. I made this remark to the chap sitting next to me, and he reassured me when he said, "The witch doctors always seem to be in the right place at the right time. It seems as if the rain they prayed for arrived, not to help us, but to help them. They must all work together, for when I was near to the West Indian supporters, groups of them keep rolling their heads, with their eyes rolling in all directions, as if demented. I'm sure this could be part of the influence." I did not disagree.

Of course there were the "ifs" about when we were fielding–if only Hick had held just one of the two chances which were offered to him, it might not have changed the result, since, for sure, our target might have been 125 or less.

My own opinion was that if the roles had been reversed and we had bowled last, and those same conditions prevailed, I could not see the frail West Indian batting lasting against Fraser, Lewis, and Caddick.

Day 8 - 5th day of 3rd Test Match

Very few people were on the coach to the ground. I was one, for I thought if it was over quickly, I could have a look round Port of Spain. It took only ten minutes to take the last two wickets, amid long sighs of relief for the few of us supporters who had braved it. Evidently, in past history England had been out for a low score of 45. The score of 46 was one of our lowest ever in any case. Curtly Ambrose had final figures of 10, 2, 24, 6...and match figures of 11 wickets for 84 runs. My own postscript: any time in future years if Curtly might be asked which Test Match did he enjoy the most, I would wager sums that it would be this one when he bowled like a demon.

I walked back to the hotel, visiting and looking in a few shop windows on the way. One thing that did strike me–just after midday–if I wanted to look round a shop, I had to ring a bell or knock to let the shopkeeper know that I was interested, and wanted to enter the premises. The reason for this was because of break-ins and robberies. Telly Kelly had warned me that I must be sure to walk on the main thoroughfares, and not to wander down side streets. Each shop was the same: a metal grille, shutters, iron bars, heavyweight doors. All had to be opened and closed within seconds of requesting an entry. I had never been shopping in these conditions, and told the owner of the place where I purchased postcards and stamps.

"Yes, I am afraid we have to do this, for here in Trinidad, and all around the island it is the same."

Mind you, travel-wise I had not been anywhere much,

1 The Emperor's Summer Palace, Beijing.

2 Part of the Great Wall of China at Ba Da Ling.

3 Bamboo sheeting protection against night frosts.

4 Near Da Ming village.

5 Bicycle repairers at Chengde.

6 On to Canada: the Victoria Glacier at Lake Louise.

7 The Fish Market, Vancouver.

8 Grouse Mountain; my camera catches the total reflection of our cable car in a huge plate glass window.

9 On to The West Indies: Scoreboard, Third Test, final day at Port of Spain, Trinidad.

10 Hibiscus in Andromeda Gardens, Barbados.

11 Joyce working on one of her crocheted pieces.

but later on in conversation with an elderly supporter about those conditions, I discovered they are commonplace in plenty of other countries.

Back at the hotel, I decided to go to my room and write a few cards. I finished at six p.m. having completed thirty, then washed and shaved, made a change of clothing. Tuna fish is on the dinner menu. Enid likes a drop of wine, and we both shared a bottle of red, which we enjoyed, and later joined Liz and John and others in the group. Nobody, it seemed, could come to terms with the result, this atmosphere continued until I left the company at eleven-thirty.

Day 9

When I arrived for breakfast each morning, the supervisor, Sally-Anne was always a very friendly person. This morning she told me that she comes to work from another part of the island in her motor, so I asked her when was it her day off: if convenient, would she like to show me round some of the island?

She replied that she was off the following day and would I be free as well? So arrangements were made for the next day at nine a.m.

I had not planned anything for today so I decided to have a walk round the Savannah or at least part of the way, passing Alfred and his taxi pals on the way down. "I told you so, Man! It was a good job Curtly did not bowl his 'quickies', man," and many similar remarks. I could only admit, "You were a better side than us," as I quickly moved past their company.

I was part of the way round the Savannah when a cloudburst arrived; shirt and shorts were my wearing apparel, so I dived for the nearest tree. This was fortunate for it was one of the giant fig trees that are a common sight around the island, enormous in both trunk and spread, this one having its candle-like flowers in bloom. I could not have been drier if I had been under a marquee—dry as a bone!

In the afternoon, I walked round to the zoo, which was in the park opposite the Savannah. I went in, had a quick look round, then the heavens opened again. I came back outside and seeing a delivery chap who I knew supplied fresh foods to the hotel, I asked if he could give me a lift to the hotel.

"Yes, jump in," he said. The rain had almost left off.

When we arrived at the long pathway, which took the walkers up, I asked the driver to drop me off just there. Thanking him, I alighted and made my way to where the termites had started their Everest climb. I quickly located the food source where people had thrown their rubbish and scraps over a parapet wall, to a sort of dried-up river bed. Here were the termites all scrambling for places in the convoy to the route back to the nest, and, of course, all uphill on a gradient of one in twenty, so loaded up they had a mighty journey back. I started counting the kerbs, and to make sure I counted correctly, for every 10 kerbs I pinpointed that particular kerb, then started again. I walked steadily upwards, with the rain beginning to fall more consistently, until I reached the point where their trail branched off, which was up an even steeper slope. I would not exaggerate if I said that this section, about ten yards in length, had a fall of one in five. The number of kerbstones was ninety. So I would not be far wrong if I said the start and finish were about 300 yards apart.

Leaning against the guard rail looking at this slope, I thought what a mess it was getting in. Now with the water streaming down this well-used three-inch wide track, it was to say the least a tiny bit slippery, yet this did not deter in the slightest any goodies being transported back up this miniature Eiger Mountain. One termite, I noticed in particular, had captured a wasp, several times bigger, and probably lugged it up from the starting point. What a struggle was going on to keep it on track! Other termites also wanted to give assistance to this piece of the action and presumably gain plaudits from those in control. This was making things worse for the hero of the moment who was very determined to go the way he wanted, regardless of where all the help was coming from. All of a sudden, a dam of broken twigs came apart owing to the water pressure building up. This sent a cascade of water pouring down which engulfed the track completely.

"What's down there, then?" a voice said, and turning round I saw one of our party under an umbrella, and quickly realising that it was pouring with rain now, I answered, "It's quite amazing, one of the termites is trying to take a wasp back to its nest, and see–it has not let go!"

"What termite nest?" I was asked.

"Up there." I pointed to the probable nest under a maple tree.

"I can see the wasp now; they are big ants, aren't they?" he said and walked off.

I was now wet right through, but had decided to walk back up by myself whilst contemplating this piece of nature that I had been witness to–the total patience, calmness, strength and bloody-mindedness of an insect, that to some people, like the chap fast disappearing up the pathway was not of the slightest interest. Yet to a minority like myself, it was a marvel to behold this one insect's daily routine for survival.

Back in my room, a nice hot shower put me back into the land of "comfort".

I wanted to get some repairs done to my banner, so after making myself presentable I walked round to where the hotel's shopping complex was. I had checked several of the shops out last night, and made straight to the shop that sold clothing. The owner had had to go out, but had left Betty, a good-natured Trinidadian seamstress, to attend to my requests. I showed her the strips of cloth in the four corners and asked her if she could lengthen and strengthen them, saying, "Make it nice and strong, so they do not pull off." This remark must have appealed to her, for she said, "Sure man, when I finish de job you could pull a battleship with it," laughing. So I had to join in too.

I had my evening meal with Mrs Spicer. My word, she is a chatty person, and while I was in her company, as most of us had noticed how her face was getting more and more crimson, and now like a beetroot colour, I thought I'd say something. "It must be painful, Enid," I offered.

"No, I use my sun lotion at the right times, and so far I am all right but I will agree, Percy, it is rather red."

I had a few drinks with the lads, but nobody has seen much of Telly Kelly, I know, like myself, he was devastated at the England result. Several are still not able to come to terms with the outcome—those upset keep making the point that we had had the best of the first three days.

Day 10

Breakfast was early, as I had to be down at the Savannah for my excursion with Sally Anne. I had only been waiting a couple of minutes when she came walking along. Wow! I thought to myself, and wanted to turn and run away. How could I think of walking along with this girl dressed in a white blouse and a pair of navy blue shorts? She quickly put me at ease when she said, "Hello, Percy, shall we have a walk round the Savannah first before our drive?"

From then onwards the ice was broken, and I felt much more at home walking beside her. Mind you, I bet we looked an odd couple for I am not ashamed to admit I have been showing my age for years now. Even now, striding out beside her, I gently had to reproach her for this speed, when I said, "You know, Sally-Anne, is there any rush, for I was going to ask you the names of some of the trees we are passing by?" This slowed the pace up dramatically, especially when she asked for the second time if the walk was too much for me.

There was no way that I could take offence at remarks like that, neither would anyone else have, come to that. If you happened to be in Sally Anne's company, it was charm and charisma—she was fairly buzzing with it and you knew that when she said things like that, it was meant in a sympathetic way.

I did mention to her that my knee played me up now and again, but that it was nothing to worry about. About two-thirds of the way round and spotting an ice-cream salesman I said, "How about an ice?"

"Yes," came the reply, "why not?" So for five minutes

we sat under one of the big fig trees enjoying the world passing by.

Sally Anne said, "Rather than go round the rest of the Savannah we can take a shortcut to where my car is parked."

I replied, "Lead on."

Arriving at her car, Sally Anne said, "It's a friend's motor, who does not look after it very well."

Looking it over, I just said, "Don't worry about that, let's go to the nearest garage and fill it up with petrol."

This was soon done, and then my excursion round part of the island began. I could not say what parts we visited, only trusting to Sally Anne's knowledge. One of the first places we stopped at was a cathedral–Queen Anne? We went inside and while we were walking round it I realised that Sally Anne was a deeply religious young lady. She did tell me what faith, but this slipped the memory. Certainly, she knew her stuff when it came to holy expressions–that was now as you can gather, and befuddling my brainbox quite a little.

When we arrived at the lectern, noticing the hymn board above it I said, "You know it's almost identical to the one in our church in the village I come from. I used to change the hymns on it."

I have no doubt my status improved in Sally Anne's estimation no end, especially when I said I used to pump the wind into the church organ as well.

There then came some rapid-fire questions: "Do you still attend chapel, how often do you go, is there a large congregation, how often a day is Communion held?"

She was just a little hurt, for I could tell by her expression, when I said, "No I don't go very often," but then when I followed this with, "I do go and work in the churchyard nearly every week," I could see her face almost light up with this remark. It improved one hundred per cent when I added, "Perhaps twice a week in the summer," and the smile that followed was a knockout.

I asked her if this was where her family came to the services.

"No, the church where my family and I go is a long way from here, but we will visit it later."

Back in the car we stopped and looked at several old buildings, which seemed to give Sally Anne a lot of pleasure for it appeared that her family went back many generations and had been involved with these places. Some two hours later we arrived at the church that her family attended. Seeing all the flowers around, I then remembered that it was Good Friday. I asked to Sally Anne, "Is it Good Friday here in Trinidad?"

"Yes, of course, this is the start of the Easter period, when we have to make a strong family presence in this church. I was here first thing this morning and all of us are going again this afternoon and again this evening."

Outside the church after we had had a walk around, she pointed in the direction that she lived. I said, "I did not realise how far you had to come to work."

Sally Anne replied, "I can get to work in about twenty minutes, but sometimes longer—it depends on the traffic."

She then drove me round to where a private estate had been built. "Quite a number of very good quality properties here," remarked Sally Anne. "This is one place on the island that has surveillance cameras. Can you see them, Percy, on top of the poles? We had better not stop here."

Shortly after this, I saw a magnificent fan palm, growing in a well-manicured garden. I said, "Do you think, Sally Anne, that I could get out and take a snap of that beauty?"

"Well be quick then, for there is a camera viewing us."

I was out and back in before she'd hardly had time to look at her watch. I had taken not one but two. One was a real stunner, the other one not quite so good. I said, "I hope they come out all right," for the weather had been, all the morning so far, sunshine all the way.

It was shortly after this that the heavens opened, the rain lashing down, so we had to park up right near another ice-cream vendor. While we were eating our lollies, she told me that her own car was being repaired, and this was only the second time she had driven this one, and asked me if I felt safe. I didn't say it but I thought she could have driven me round all day, I would not have cared a jot. All I said was, "I have felt quite safe all the while."

We made a few more stops after the sun had come through, finally saying our goodbyes, when she dropped me off at the entrance to the zoo, both of us saying, "See you tomorrow."

I spent the rest of the afternoon dodging showers inside the zoo. The one here in Port of Spain is quite hilly with steps climbing up to cages built on different levels, so that when you reached the top, you could look out over the whole zoo, and see most of the action. This was fortunate for me, as I had climbed up during some showers and now I sat on a seat eating another ice, and recapping my good fortunes of the morning. Out of the corner of my eye, I noted two iguanas playing around the surface roots of two eucalyptus trees, no doubt looking for scraps. I suppose I was acting a bit silly, as they were again among the first I had seen in their natural habitat, for I had left my seat and was now only a few feet from them. A family of Trinidadians came along, and one lady said to me, "What has taken your interest, mister? It's surely not those pests under the trees."

I said, "It sure is, they are quite big, aren't they?"

"We have hundreds of them where we come from in St James, and they eat food from your hand, man," another said. And with this last remark, they all laughed as they strolled off. I remember seeing some in Regent's Park Zoo when I was at school and am sure they never had colouring like these two, both about the size of big rats, with tails twice as long as their bodies. I found these Trinidadian ones fascinating, for, as they knew I had an interest in them, so they came closer and closer. I was even contemplating giving them the remains of my cornet, when some lads came along kicking a football, and they disappeared in a flash.

Back down to the restaurant, I had a cold drink and watched a long rain shower pass by whilst studying the map of the layout of the zoo and gardens. It appeared to join up with the public gardens next door, and as this was in the direction of the hotel, so I decided that now the sun had come through again I would have a wander round there.

I took a photo of another type of fig tree that was growing in a dried-up gully, may even have been a dried up stream, unusual to say the least. It appeared not to have a trunk, for it had a large root system, almost twenty feet long, about ten of these with a thickness of six inches going straight into the ground—a most weird appearance.

Back in the hotel, I made up my diary for the day, washed and changed, had dinner, a few beers with the lads, knowing it was going to be one not to be forgotten in a hurry.

Day 11

I had my breakfast, and then decided to walk right round the Savannah, still giving me ample time to come back and pack my suitcase ready for our departure at four-forty-five this afternoon. Partway round I noticed a large house open to the public. This proved to be very interesting for it contained a collection of steel band instruments. The young lady convinced me the steel drums on display were the very first ones to be played anywhere in the Caribbean. These drums had been played before large audiences all over the world, and now they had come back to be looked after and cherished, and immortalised for everyone forever. Photographs of world-famous drummers in different rooms—my word, this Trinidadian young lady certainly knew her stuff. Back at the hotel I finished my packing, then went straight up to the desk to square up my account, the difference being a considerable amount paid to me in Trinidadian dollars (little did I know how much worry this transaction would cause me).

The plane left for Grantly Adams Airport, Barbados right on schedule, arriving at six p.m. I was quickly through customs, then on a coach connection to the Barbados Hilton.

After we had checked in at the desk, I wandered through the foyer, and looked round in amazement, for it was just like a miniature nature reserve. The first thing that drew my attention was the stately coconut palm that swept upwards almost to the ceiling and roof level. Six floors, I thought right away–it's got to be sixty feet at least. I left my bags and walked over to investigate. A pool of water ran into a miniature waterfall, and cascaded down some rocks for maybe eight feet. All this was covered with various sorts of plant-life, with two more coconut palms starting their climb, and looking upwards to the first-floor balconies. From here, a stairway swept down in gentle curves to where I was standing totally lost in the admiration of it all. Casting my eye upwards and round, all the floors had been planned carefully, with the balcony so designed that everyone had a chance sooner or later to acknowledge this splendid spectacle.

On entering my room on the third floor, I walked right through to another balcony, this time with sea views–the harbour, with large and small vessels of all descriptions. Yes, the hotel here at Needham Point was extraordinary to say the least.

Each of the next eleven mornings, we–well those who were that way inclined–had a dawn chorus to listen to. It was only the one bird, a wren–I have not a shadow of a doubt. Not once did I see it, but it was high up in the foliage of the coconut palm, where it had a spread of several metres. At time when you were standing outside the door of the room listening to notes only a wren can conjure up, the acoustics had to be witnessed to be believed.

There was only one person in our group who heard it, and she said, "It's a recording." I did not want to believe this, for I had got to the stage, often waking up with a sore head, when I was all expectant for the songster to herald in a new day, I know I said at the time, "Full marks to the architect, and may he design many more buildings along these lines."

Day 12

I had noticed a restaurant called The Pebbles on the hotel's approach road, so I decided to have a walk down to see what it was like, as the prices for meals in the hotel restaurant were certainly not going to suit my budget. Its prices were much more to my pocket's liking, so I decided to have all my future breakfasts here and evening meals in the hotel.

Walking back beside the seashore that leads along past our hotel, I found that even as early as this the sea was full of swimmers. Back up to the room I picked up what I needed, suntan oil, etc., and made my way through the foyer which led straight to the beach. Magic! Spotting a nice dwarf palm which gave a nice amount of shade, I spread out my bath towel, covered up with oils and then I was in and out of the water three or four times—each time back to the shade of the palm tree. I had to move my gear three times as the sun was moving round incredibly quickly, and each time I came back out of the water the sun had moved my towel from the shade into full treatment of its powers. I had been warned not to lie in the sun between ten a.m. and two p.m. as the temperature does more harm then than at any time during the day. About noon I packed up, had a cold drink from the bar on the beach, and went back to my room.

I was to room-share with Martin, a chap from Coventry, who I had not met but had corresponded with. He was due to arrive with the next group of Mike Burton England cricket supporters, on Wednesday 6th, and seemed to have a good knowledge of the game.

In the afternoon I walked down to the main road and caught a taxi-bus, the charge one and a half dollars. This took me right into Bridgetown. I discover whilst on the taxi-bus that it does not matter where you hail it from en-route, the fare is always the same amount, whatever direction it has come from or is going to—I had not a clue, I do know at times it was packed.

There were quite a number of different tour groups about here in Bridgetown, so I was sure that when our main party joined us, the England cricket team was sure of plenty of support. My word, it was hot, and much hotter than in Trinidad; my legs seemed to be at times on fire, I looked at them several times, and thought they ought not to be that colour. I could not understand it, for I had put sun cream on according to the maker's recommendations.

Finding a supermarket, I went in and purchased a dozen fresh rolls, a tub of butter, two packets of cheese slices and a carton of milk for the sum of nine dollars. As soon as I got home I would put them straight in the fridge in the room.

Here in Bridgetown I was to find, as in most of the places in Trinidad, that you had a job to locate the taxi-bus you required, for there was nothing to put you in the direction you wanted to travel.

I never saw any tickets on these short journeys. The vehicles were licensed to carry ten people. Every journey I made this number of passengers was always exceeded by another five adults, or if there were children, this might even be another fifteen. When I went back this first time I had arrived late, and the taxi-bus was just leaving. I was found a seat in the back, so I had to send my money to the conductor, or collector (just a coloured shirt and shorts) via three passengers, and then my change came back the same route. After my christening in this transaction, I always had the right money available.

What I had straightaway noticed was the happy atmosphere that prevailed amongst the travelling company; nobody seemed to mind about time—if you did not arrive on time, you would arrive sometime, and if you didn't arrive today then whatever the job it had to wait until tomorrow. As you joined in conversation, you found tomorrow never came, so it was just hard luck for anyone's programme.

I did wonder at times, and even on this trip back to the hotel, about the amount of small business that seemed to be normally transacted on these taxi-buses. Opposite me now was two very large Barbadian women, carrying large colourful bags; inside—your guess is as good as mine. I don't know to this day what was inside. The person sitting beside me said when I asked what was being carried, "They is washing, man."

I was later to find out from an insider from the inside that the purpose of this is to avoid paying any licence fees. If a business is to survive, this is the only way, so they carry their work round with them. All the business around the island are organised like this, and all the officials are satisfied with this method of bargaining.

Back in my room, I had a shower, and when I stripped off, I was amazed to find my chest and right leg looked as if they had been fried. I was mighty pleased that I had left the beach when I did, for if I had stayed another half an hour I would have been cooked properly. I told John and Liz later how I sat under a palm tree and got sunburnt. "That wants some believing, getting burnt through the leaves, they are quite thick," said John.

"I can't believe it myself, but here's the proof," I replied, showing them my leg.

Day 13

John and Liz had now joined me at breakfast at the Pebbles Restaurant, where Dulcie the waitress was making sure that the English visitors were made welcome and looked after, always with a nice smile.

There was a race meeting up at the Savannah this afternoon. We all agreed to meet each other for the first. "Where are you off to then, Perc?" John asked.

"I am going down to Bridgetown to find a bus that will take me to a place called Bethsheba," I said.

"What's there?" Liz asked.

"It's a garden which is open to the public, called the Andromeda Gardens–see you later." Catching the taxi-bus to the terminus, I was then pointed in the direction of where all the buses arrive and depart to all over the island. What a bit of luck! One was leaving in five minutes. I paid my fare, asking the driver if he would put me off at the Andromeda Gardens. "Yes, certainly, it takes about half an hour," the driver replied helpfully. I thanked him and was soon on my way.

About the bus–I am quite sure that when the bus started its life on these Barbadian roads the springs would have been in excellent condition, but now, a few years maybe down the line, those pieces of comfort were practically non-existent. I was sitting on the back seat, and almost directly over the wheel arches, so you can imagine what it was like going over the frequent and not so tiny pot-holes. Now and again I would turn my head and look behind to see how wide and deep the offending hole was.

Even I was surprised at times to see some a foot deep, and perhaps two to three feet wide.

As we progressed across the island, these potholes became more and more numerous, and what did not improve matters were the wooden slatted seats. Sitting next to me were two children, over six and under ten, together with their mum, most everyone in fits of laughter as each one hung on for dear life to stop themselves from falling off the seats. I thought at the time that the gangway down the middle need not have been so wide, then they could have put in another row of seats, though this would not have made any difference to the comfort.

The two children had been trying to engage me in conversation for some time, and at last the older one said to me in quite a loud voice, "Why are you here, and who are you visiting?"

A deadly quietness came over the entire bus. In a very soft voice, which was hardly audible even to me, I said, "I am an England cricket supporter."

It was loud enough for the whole bus of some thirty people to burst out laughing. The children's mum had to get out her hankie to wipe the tears from both her eyes. There had been joviality before on the bus, but now there was jubilation, everyone stamping their feet, and those who were quiet before my whispered confession of being a true Brit were not now.

At close range, I had questions fired at me from all seats. "What, man, did you say?" "Who is them English supporters?" "Are you going home early, man?" "Brian, he beat you on his own." And lots and lots more. Thankfully the driver called out, "Andromeda Gardens."

I bade them all goodbye and as I stood waiting for the

bus to depart, the driver said, "Bus goes back every half hour."

As I looked up at the departing bus, all the passengers were standing up waving at me, including two children in the back seat, right until it was out of sight.

I looked all round. I was standing on a fairly steep hill, with no sign of any gardens, so guessing they were down the road I started walking, then seeing a couple sitting in the shade of a dwarf palm, I asked them if they could tell me in what direction they were. "Not far down the hill on the right."

"Many thanks," my reply.

Asking the time of a chap in the car park, it was ten-forty-five, so I thought I could have three hours here, allow half an hour on the bus, be at the races well before the first race at three p.m. I had been told that the Andromeda Gardens enjoyed a healthy relationship with the National Trust back in England, so joining the queue to get in, I showed the old gentleman my NT card who said, "You over here from England?"

"Yes," I replied.

He went on, "Whenever I visit the old country, any places that have NT status, I show my membership card, like you are doing here."

Now I had got my ticket for entry, I decided to search out a cuppa. No luck, I had to make do with an ice-cream. I sat inside on a seat, taking particular notice right away of how lush everywhere was. And not a lot of breathing space for plants, shrubs or trees.

It was not long before the old chap found me, soon telling me what areas to look for that might interest me, saying that most of the specimens had been purchased and brought there from all parts of the world. "Be careful in some parts as the paths are quite slippery owing to the moisture dripping from the trees; this is important for several of the species you will see as you walk round."

I thought of the five or six old ladies that I worked for in my redeployed occupation, and how they would have been overjoyed to see some of the plants and shrubs I tended and cared for here in their natural surroundings. For instance, back home, I knew offhand of three gardens that had bougainvillaea. In one place here they had been left to grow in a natural state, even could have been uncultivated, certainly they were not looked after. As I looked across to try to take a photo, not only did I have to hold my breath whilst clicking the shutter, but continued to do so as I took in all the multitude of colours. There was no way that I could avoid the sun, which was directly in front of me and quite bright. The thought went through my mind not to let the folk back home down, which I would if I could not back up what I'd seen with what I had seen in the flesh—the purples of six different shades, perhaps at least fifteen colours. My diary states: "A myriad of coloration."

Continuing along this high side of the gardens, I came across another apparition, this time hibiscus, a trial garden no less with maybe fifty different hybrids and as I looked closely at each bloom, not one was of the same hue or tint colouring. I was bending down to make sure I was going to get a good shot with my camera when a voice said, "What do you think of these?" Turning round, the old chap was standing there. He then gave me a good education in cross pollination, really baffling me with all his experience and knowledge, he not doubting for one minute the person so enthralled was a very green specimen, unlikely to scratch the plant world with so much as one thumbful acquired over the years. You could see he slept, ate, and drank plants of every denomination.

I said to him as soon as he had stopped to take a breath, "I am very sorry to tell you, I am an avid listener, but my knowledge is very limited, and I don't profess to know too much about the hows, whys and wherefores, et cetera. I am just an interested person who likes to see how a person like yourself ticks. I have been in the building trade for over forty years. I like to see how you achieve wonders like these hibiscus we are now looking at.

Another face I shall not forget in a hurry, his weatherbeaten one gradually broke into a grin which spread from ear to ear, saying, "You could have fooled me!"

I took some more photos while he was telling me more about these hybrid hibiscus, but certainly not with the same enthusiasm. Each of them were stem grafts taken from all parts of the globe. I always presumed, after this frank admission on my part, that he had seen my National Trust membership card and assumed that I was an informed authority who could converse with his own grey cells.

I came across a very unusual tree, (again) a gardener was cleaning round the roots, very similar to the one I had seen in Trinidad. These surface roots were some six feet from the ground; it was no doubt another type of fig tree. I asked Benjamin if I could take a photo of him with the tree. He told me he was one of two gardeners who worked here, and yes he very much liked his job.

After asking him the time, I realised that by the time I

got over to the entrance, and had a cuppa, it would be time to catch my bus back to Bridgetown.

It did not matter where you walked or stopped to observe a plant or shrub, you would notice a movement in the grass or vegetation–always an iguana, some quite small. Again, I tried my hardest to get them to sit still for my photo shoot, but no such luck–as soon as you attempted to make a move, they were gone.

I had my beverage and, walking out to the highway for the bus, I remembered I had admired the entrance when I came in, so decided to take a photo of the three-foot high bougainvillaea hedges, again multi-coloured. They made the wooden arched entrance design very charming, leading into this rectangular garden neatly laid out with lawns and beds full of annuals.

The old chap popped up again, asking me if I had enjoyed my visit, to which I replied that I most certainly had.

For the next few minutes I was again given words of wisdom, and it soon became clear that he was also seeking some ideas for improvements to some of the buildings that no doubt I had seen as I walked round. I told him certainly some of the work required on several timber buildings needed a vast amount of money spent, but would suggest that the cheapest thing to do would be to demolish them."

Though this logical approach did not meet with his approval, I could see that his mind was certainly miles away from the Andromeda Gardens and its plant life.

"I look forward to seeing you in the not too distant future," and with a good firm handshake, I was away to catch my transport.

Something that the old chap had said reminded me that today was Easter Monday, and when I was in the garden's cafeteria, and looking at the large map on the wall, I had noticed that at Bethsheba, down the hill, it appeared to have a large sandy beach, so it was just like home. Everyone on the bus was going to the seaside. At this time, it should not be so busy as on the journey coming out.

This proved to be correct when the bus arrived just after one p.m. with very few on the vehicle, and twenty minutes later I was at the racetrack. As I mingled with the crowds, it seemed they were not only local people from around the island, but had also been flown in from the many islands in the Caribbean for this day at the races. I gathered this information from a local chap I was talking to as I waited to put on my dollars for my first bet. One of my three lucky numbers is three, I could see that the start of the race was imminent and by the time I had completed reading how to place my bet, the bell rang and the window closed. Too late! The tapes went up, and coming past me in the lead was No 3 who duly won at odds of 5 to 1. In between races you could cross over to the inside of the track, so I did, always keeping an eye open for John and Liz and ·Telly Kelly: no luck–which also applied to the race card.

What I did discover was that it was mighty hot here, and I tried to find the shade all the time. I was glad I had put plenty of oils on my painful parts before I had left the hotel this morning. I had a look at them now and again, none of the brighter red ones looked any different, so there must have been an improvement taking place.

As well as racing, lots of entertainment was taking place with celebrities by the score. I noticed Sir Gary Sobers again, but only from a distance, and wherever he or other personalities were, a crowd of autograph hunters would descend on them, mostly children, it appeared. I had had quite a few ice creams, and as soon as the last race was finished and I had not backed a winner from all the six races, I decided to go back to the hotel. It was less than a mile and past the Garrison, I had done a fair bit of walking today. Back in the room the first thing I looked at was my body parts, pleased to see that they were now, instead of the beetroot red, a quieter shade of claret.

Meeting up with Liz and John later, they asked me where I had got to. I told them of my day excursion, and that I had looked for them at the races, but could not locate them. I asked them what plans they had for tomorrow.

"How about you, where are you going?" both asked.

"I thought of going to Harrison's Caves."

"Oh, how do we get there, and what's the attraction at Harrison Caves?" Liz asked.

"I don't know myself, only that they are world famous as caves go," I replied.

Telly Kelly had now come back to join us, and was also interested in coming along, and by now the time was almost eleven-thirty p.m. We all agreed to see each other in the morning and find out what Harrison Caves were and where.

Day 14

I went down to the Pebbles, and finding that I was now getting on quite well with Dulcie, and the three poached eggs were done just as I like them, I asked her if she drove a car. "Yes, I do drive and I own one." I then suggested to her that when she had a day off, she might like to show me round part of the Island.

She replied, "You will have to ask the boss, as he determines which and what day I have off."

"That's mean; I should have thought you would have a certain day, or two regular ones off each week."

"Jobs are hard to find here in Barbados, so we have to accept the conditions, and he is a very good boss and treats us girls very well. Often we have dinner parties, and now the cricketers are here it get very busy," she replied.

All ready for our day's at ten a.m. we all caught the taxi-bus down to Bridgetown, which takes about ten minutes. As for the weather, it had the appearance of being a scorcher, with each of us wearing the right gear, and all in a jovial mood.

The bus left for Harrison Caves at ten-thirty and this time I was not the only one who saw the funny side of sitting on the slatted seats. They caused a lot of amusement to my company who agreed this was the first time for ages that they had sat on anything like these. Again the bus was made up chiefly of local Barbadians, full of spirits, and laughter, they made you feel you had to laugh along with them, and if you didn't you seemed out of place. I daresay in retrospect, it was us the majority was laughing at, but who cared.

Telly Kelly says it's eleven o'clock: we will soon be there, if the driver is right when he told us it would take half an hour. Five minutes later the driver calls out, "Harrison's Caves." John asked him if the caves were down the hill and how far.

"Ten minutes walk, you can't miss them," the driver said.

"What time does the bus go back to Bridgetown?" Telly Kelly asked.

"Every half hour," he called out, closing the doors, "the bus stop is just along the road."

We all agreed that the ten minutes was nearer twenty than ten. At the entrance to Harrison's Caves we had to join a queue of people waiting to enter, so we did what most people were doing, purchased a ticket, fifteen dollars, then while waiting for the numbers to be called, away for a bite to eat and a nice cool beer.

We waited for about twenty minutes, and then an electric battery-operated train arrived, pulling six trucks, each holding four adults or according to people's size. The truck in front of ours held two adults and four children, and an infant as well. John at the time said in a quiet voice, "I bet it's only a few days old."

As we went from the brilliant sunshine to almost complete darkness in one go, for a few minutes it seemed very strange whilst our eyes were getting used to the caves' atmosphere and its secrets. We found that rubber tyres over a very smooth tarred macadam surface also gave us a very comfortable ride. In most caves I have visited, not a lot of lighting has been apparent, or so I had witnessed, but this one was certainly different, for everywhere we drove, along the walls, and overhead, tube lighting was the norm, like miniature tube tunnels.

We had all been kitted out with hard hats, and for myself mine turned out to be a blessing in disguise, later on during our drive round.

Every now and again we stopped for camera shots, and for the experts this was just the job. All the lighting effects, because of where they were concealed, gave those snappers excellent positions, without leaving the vehicle. I have never, and for that matter I don't suppose I ever will go to "Fairyland", and as our tour continued this to me was getting more and more feasible! I suppose I was getting carried away with this underground exhibition of concealment, of fluorescent tubes, bulbs, and the like when, "Mind your head, Perc," and Telly Kelly grabbed me, pulling me back into the truck. I looked back and up to see a piece of overhanging rock sticking out twenty inches or more; this would have given my helmet a real testing. "Thanks, Telly," I said. He replied, "That's another beer you owe me."

Gliding over the roadway made the silence even more uncanny, for, except for the water dripping and the odd cough or two, there was no sound. In the tunnels we were travelling through, an outstretched hand horizontally or vertically could have touched the walls at any time.

I am sure it was the absence of noise that made this all the more enthralling. I was facing forward, so I could see what was going to arrive round the next bend. When we arrived at a cavern called the Great Hall, this was very sudden and took me by surprise and everybody else too judging by the "Aah, Aahs". The driver and guide told us that it is something like fifty feet high and sixty feet wide, so it will give you an idea of the size we were all taking in. Stalactites coming down from the ceiling of the Great Hall seemed awesome in their size and magnificence. Breathtaking is not a generous enough word, for you could not bring your eye to focus on one alone. Their length I could not hazard a guess at, and from the cavern floor there were stalagmites too. Hardly anyone spoke above a whisper, for the whole ensemble seemed to have a hallowed air abounding, and then, to crown this magical vibration, the baby started crying.

It did not matter what the parents did to pacify the tiny infant, he or she made sure the noise continued unabated. By now the transport had stopped for us all to stretch our legs and I, for one, was glad of this as my limbs were beginning to stiffen up. Telly Kelly, seeing I was having a job to reach terra firma some eighteen inches below, jumped out and steadied me on the way down, saying, "That's two beers you owe me already."

We only stopped here for five minutes but it was long enough to realise that this was an unforgettable experience. Back in the transport there were several of the passengers quietly whispering about the baby and saying, "The parents ought to know better," or, "Fancy having a baby on board," or "Why didn't they leave it with someone?" and more.

For some time, from the seat I was sitting in, I could see a tiny stream that had been following us wherever we went. It did not matter what level we were travelling over, high or low, it was always there beside me. At times I could have reached out and touched it with my hand. Then, already going very slowly, the transport stopped and I was to see at first-hand that the channel with the water flowing through was a man-made one of an identical limestone colouring. Casting my eye upwards, I noticed a long fluorescent tube concealed from view, and this in turn was giving everything its magical effect.

The baby continued to cry for the rest of the twenty minutes we were in Harrison Caves. Before long we were going up a gentle gradient, to arrive back in daylight–and the baby stopped straightaway.

I often wondered, at such an early age, is darkness a thing?

Next—a chance to view a short video about the island. This was always a must for me, because it tells you what you least expect and usually has surprises in store.

Barbados, the eastern-most part of all the islands in the Caribbean, has a population of approximately 250,000 people. As for the name Barbados, it is still not clear how it was so named. Some say Los Barbados (the Bearded One) as a bearded Portuguese discovered the island in 1536. The island is made up of limestone, and wherever you walk it is just under the surface, and runs for hundreds of feet. Harrison's Caves have been open to the public since 1981, with safety and improvements always ongoing programmes. On the ground above the caves, breadfruit and palm trees are some of the lime-loving genre that abound across the island, together with white cedar, mahogany, citrus trees, banana plantations, just a few of the large foliage specimens that help to make up the environment. Stalactites and stalagmites form in the most unusual places. If you see water dripping and you are able to remove some of the covering flora and fauna, what wonderment is in store! Some parts around the island will surely amaze you with creations made over thousands upon thousands of years, and, looking at some of the formations on the screen, they are tremendous.

The final caption came up: "We trust you have enjoyed your visit, and look forward to seeing you again in the future."

Another beer, and we decided to make tracks for Bridgetown, I was asked if I could negotiate a deal with the numerous taxi drivers that were looking for trade. None seemed interested in the terms I was offering.

There then followed a quick committee meeting, and we all agreed that we go back the same way as we had come, so we walked back to the bus stop directly opposite the one we alighted from in the morning. We waited there, I was informed by those wearing a watch, for half an hour. Then another five minutes passed and some local people, who had passed us earlier were now returning. One called out, "If you are waiting for de bus, you am waiting in de wrong place."

None of us could believe this: the locals across the road had now been joined by three more and, of course, our misfortunes had been conveyed to the newcomers. Each and every one was now laughing their heads off and one stoutish lady was bent over double. Seeing this, we were obliged to join in as well.

Finally, when order had been reasonably restored, an elderly man called out, "The bus you want is up the hill and to the right. You will see it in the distance, the colour is blue."

"Many thanks," we all said.

Sure thing after walking up the incline and turning into a banana- and palm-tree-edged road, there was the bus right at the very end of the road. I would say without exaggeration, it was a good quarter of a mile away.

On boarding and paying our fares, the driver then said, "We will be leaving in fifteen minutes," and continued chatting to two other passengers. Now we were on board, and sitting at the back of the bus, we were, no doubt, the centre of conversation, and there was lots of laughing.

This was the sort of situation I was to find myself in as I explored the island over the next few days. If you found yourself at a bus stop, and a bus came along and did not stop, most likely it was to another destination on the island. There was nothing on any bus to say where it had come from, or where it was going to, and for that matter nothing on the bus stop sign, like the one by this particular bus.

After fifteen minutes, John went along and made enquiries and was told by one of the driver's two buddies that the driver was now having his twenty-minute tea break, because he had made good time coming up from Bridgetown. All this we could hear from the back of the bus. We then heard him tell John that if we walked back to where the bus stop was on the hill, one was due there (the driver looking at his watch) in ten minutes.

Another committee meeting to review our position, and we concluded unanimously that as we had parted with out fare money, we would stay put.

By the time the bus did start up, another twenty-five minutes had passed, making it an hour and twenty minutes that had passed since we arrived at the bus stop on the hill. By now, another ten passengers had joined the rest of us.

On the way to Bridgetown we picked up quite a bit of local trade, each new passenger stepping aboard being briefed about the foreigners sitting at the back. Then someone guessed right about us, and then the welcome to those boarding was, "They are some of the mad English cricket supporters." This remark would bring about huge peals of laughter all along the bus. We barely spoke, just joined in with laughing along with them and this good humour continued right through to the terminus.

Alighting from the bus, a visit to the Fisherman's Arms was the first stop on the agenda for several of the group had said this place was the "bee's knees". Up two flights of wrought-iron staircase and inside, and the time now four p.m. "It's as busy now as when it first opened," one of the barmen said, when asked if they closed at all. "It's like this all day long."

Telly Kelly ordered some sandwiches; given the time we waited for this to arrive, Telly Kelly remarked, "I think they have run out of food, and are borrowing some from elsewhere!" We had almost given up when it duly arrived and yes, they were well worth waiting for.

A large supermarket nearby was out next port of call and this was quite close to the taxi-bus, so we did not have to travel far with our purchases. We all were of the same opinion that bottles of drink were the most important buy. Laden down with various assortments, we found our taxi-bus that delivered us to the end of the road leading to our hotel. It was not too far to walk, time now five-forty-five p.m. and then, "See you later," for management was putting on drinks and cocktails up at the old fort at six-thirty.

Showered, shaved, and presentable, I arrived at six-forty-five to find that almost every guest who was a patron of the hotel was present, and was quickly informed, "You have to be quick, Perc, for the freebies will disappear in no time." This person was quite right, for it was down the hatch in minutes!

It seemed that the old fort where we were having this do (adjoining the hotel) had been quickly established by the English when they arrived here in 1627 to protect the island against any invader who showed warlike intentions. This must have been an excellent position for it is the furthest piece of land on Needham's Point, which overlooks Carlisle Bay. Every few yards there is a cannon positioned, and looking down twenty feet or more to the depths below, gave you an insight into the difficult task anyone faced who wanted to try their luck with all this artillery. No doubt, the wise ones kept away.

The Island of Barbados gained its independence in 1966.

Complete darkness had now fallen, and all around us was illuminated, including the big ships out in the bay; it all seemed so perfect, mindless of the terrible deeds executed through history.

The evening became more and more friendly and amicable; we were all strangers to each other despite all coming from the old country–Dave and Gerald, Jan and Bill, John and Liz, to name but a few. However, I was to find, as the days progressed, that the camaraderie of everyone was a delight. We were all here for a good time, enjoy each other's company, and, most important, I was to find, give our cricketers plenty of vocal support.

Day 15

Early breakfast, just after seven-forty-five a.m., back to the hotel room to pick up my towel, et cetera. for the beach. This morning the sea was churning out some big rollers, so I did not venture in too far. I had noticed that both my knees were getting more difficult to bend, I was very surprised that this was occurring, for my doctor had convinced me that the sun would work wonders on my old bones, yet so far I have yet to find the benefits of these very hot conditions. I remember someone else saying, "Your body will be more supple and manoeuvrable." This is also far from being the case.

The water here is just as the postcards suggest. The beach, sky and sea are exactly what it portrays. I did not stay long as I wanted to go down to Bridgetown to sort my money out. When I had left the hotel in Trinidad, the balance of my travellers' cheques had been given back to me in Trinidadian dollars, something like 1,500 dollars of their currency, and here in Barbados I was having the dickens of a job to find anyone who I could do business with. I had so far been managing to change a travellers' cheque to negotiate transactions, but as soon as I asked for a Trinidad dollar to be exchanged for Barbados ones it was, "Very sorry." Even the hotel reacted in this way.

Before I left I located the manager, who I suspect had heard about the guest who was trying to find him to seek an explanation as to why he was having all this bother with their currency. I heard he was with the concierge, so straightaway I asked him why I could not have my Trinidadian dollars exchanged.

His reply was, "Very sorry, but if you go down to the bank in Bridgetown you will get them changed, no problem."

I said to him, "I have already made my mind up to go down there, but thought you would oblige." There was just a shrug of his shoulders, as he said so that I hardly heard, "I wish both countries could be friends." It did not mean a thing to me at the time.

I got the key to the safe, collected the dollars and made my way down to the taxi-bus. It was not long before one came along, and I asked the driver on boarding, if he could drop me off near a bank. This the driver duly obliged me by doing, just before the terminus.

First, the Barbados National Bank: walking in I went straight to Information, explained to the young lady what business I wanted transacting, so she pointed me to one of several cash points, where I explained why I wanted to change my Trinidad dollars. Without any hesitation on her part the cashier said, "You have come to the wrong bank, you want the Commonwealth Bank the next street over."

When I arrived there, it was the same story again. They told me to try Barclays Bank—yes, they would certainly make an exchange. Back to the main part of Bridgetown; here at least, when I was refused help, they did give me a possible reason for all the banks' attitude. "Well sir, it is because we do not have a very good working relationship with Trinidad and Tobago, and so we do not have anything to do with their currency. However, there are three more banks which might help you," and with this I was given a piece of paper showing where I was to find them.

As I had put my name down for an excursion to an Open House do at Chummery St James for early afternoon, I decided to pack this wild goose chase up and go back to the hotel for a wash and brush-up to make myself presentable.

The coach arrived at one-thirty p.m. picking up several other visitors to the island who, like myself, were curious as to life in rural areas. A lady came and sat beside me, so we introduced each other, she telling me her name was Sylvia, and determined to leave her other half on the beach in a deckchair. It appears like me, she was very interested in looking round this private estate. Finally, about ten people were on board, all of different nationalities except the two of us.

The property and the grounds were indeed open to all, for as you listened to the various chatter we both agreed many different languages were being used.

You could investigate inside and outside the house–they were brave people to let perfect strangers stroll wherever something took their fancy. The mansion, as somebody described it, was a four-up and four-down dwelling and only one room was barred from entry; if you so wished you could partake in free drinks, of rum, whisky and mixes. This was in exchange for a ticket we had received on our entry to the property. A couple who I had been talking to as we walked round asked me if I would like their tickets. Very seldom do I refuse an offer of this nature, and with a "many thanks" I had a double recharge.

Quite quickly I found myself in conversation with the chap who was looking after the bar, and the disposal of the nectar; he also happened to be the owner of this paradise.

He asked me where I came from in the United Kingdom, and I told him I was from Essex. His response to this was, "Well I'm blowed, I used to live in Debden near Loughton. I sold up many years ago and purchased this place, and have been restocking with plants for the garden ever since. Whereabouts in Essex do you live?"

When I told him I was from High Beech just about three miles from Debden he said, "Yes, I know it well. I used to go for a drink in Dick Turpin's Cave. Is it still there?" continuing, "How do you spell High Beech, with one 'e' or two?"

I answered, "The amount of times I have been asked the same question! I'll tell you how I have informed the other enquirers. Our family used to run the local post office for well over half a century and the two previous families who had it before that, before 1843, all spelt it with the two 'e's'."

To this he replied, "I have got no answer to that, I give in."

Sylvia had now found me, and the owner asked us both if we would like another glass for old times, and until we meet again. As we all continued talking, he reminded me very much of the old chap at Andromeda Gardens–a lot of knowledge accumulated over a long life. I asked him if I could take a photo of him, but this he declined saying, "Anywhere in the garden, tree, shrub, plant, or the cats, but please leave me out."

Back on the coach, as we were arriving near to the dropping off points, Sylvia, knowing that I was with a travel group of cricket supporters, like herself and her husband Bob, asked if I would come in and meet him when we arrived at her hotel. "Yes of course," I said.

We found him quickly, and after the introductions he said he had been sunbathing. There followed a brief discussion on what changes, if any should be made to the proposed line-up for the test match starting tomorrow. We said cheerio, promising to meet the day after next at the test match. Arriving back at the hotel, I was told that my room-mate had arrived and taken the key–and what a fine chap Martin turned out to be.

He told me he had had a decent flight over and wanted to know about the test match in Trinidad. I told him I felt sure the West Indies had the rub of the green when we played there.

That evening was one I will remember for a very long time. Martin had joined me in having our evening meal. Afterwards, I told him that if he wanted to join the other members who I had made friends with, he would be made most welcome. He said, "I'll pop down later on."

It appeared as if the rest of the Mike Burton outfit had now arrived at the Hilton, so the place was buzzing with cricket supporters, and another tour leader, Julie, had come with them. I then searched Julie out, and, of course, the first words she said to me were, "I have been looking forward to meeting you, as I was in the office back in England hearing all about your misfortunes. I also put all your travel papers together, and it clearly stated Heathrow Airport to pick up WIAA!"

I explained again for the umpteenth time what I had done and then I asked her if she could do me a favour. Julie said, "Yes of course, that's what we are here for."

I then explained to her about my Trinidadian dollars, how when I had left the Hilton at Port of Spain they had given me their currency. She replied, "I can't believe that!" and clearly did not realise that Trinidad and Tobago are not the best of friends with Barbados.

Julie then said, "What I will try to do tomorrow is try a few other banks, and if I don't have any joy I will take them off you and give you the same value in Barbadian dollars."

"What will you do with them if you can't change them?" I asked.

"I will take them home and change them in my bank," she said.

"Thanks very much, I will be grateful as they have been a constant worry to me for some time."

I suppose there were about eighteen or so people in one of the bars, when a Karaoke started. The sheets with all the songs came round, and as a few were joining in and putting their names down, so I was persuaded to put mine down. It was very similar to the one in I had got myself involved with in Canada, the difference being there was only a handful of people here against the crowded bar in Vancouver.

Mind you, Mike Burton's new arrivals were quickly getting used to the rum and mixes, around in another part of the establishment.

My turn soon came round, the DJ saying, "Percy, it's your turn."

My choice, an old song called "You are my sunshine" was completed with a fair bit of applause. The DJ said, "After all the Karaoke singers have completed their songs, I will present a bottle of rum to the person who receives the most applause."

An hour later and now the support had risen to some forty people. Yes, I won the bottle but that was down to the Mike Burton outfit collectively. I told those sitting nearby, "We will crack it one evening."

It was now well past midnight, and quite a few I could see would need help to somewhere.

Day 16

Breakfast down at the Pebbles Restaurant, and my room-mate Martin now having fully recovered his land legs, has decided to come with me for a bus ride. I have told him that I have not been to the far north of the island yet, and thought about exploring that today. "Fine, I don't mind," he said.

Down to the bus depot, we enquire about the bus to Speightstown, where we would have to change for another to a place called Pye Corner, then waiting ten minutes for our bus to leave. Martin from Coventry is in the motor trade, and when first seeing the bus, its interior and wooden seats, remarked, "Oh, my God!" This journey was like my other ones—over very rough country. When we made our change to another service, this bus, lo and behold, had a form of leather upholstery, but unfortunately it was placed directly over the wooden slats, so although it looked nice and comfortable, this in no way helped the agony our posteriors were going through. We had now left the main road and were going into sugar-cane plantation areas, with now and again citrus fruit, and bread fruit trees which I had now come to recognise. Where fields of sugar cane had been harvested, tractors were already ploughing and preparing for the next season's crops. My word, looking across, you could hardly see the machines for the dust that arose from the plough-shares, but there was something very much like home here—seagulls following the plough.

We arrived at a place, that from the bleakness and foreboding of the surroundings should have been called No Man's Land. We looked along the bus to find there were only two passengers, Martin and myself. The driver stopped for just a couple of minutes, checked his till, then turning in a large circle, we entered the same road we had come up on. Both of us almost in one voice said, "This must be the end of the line."

We had hardly voiced this opinion when the bus stopped and the driver walked down the bus towards us and said, "Can I see your tickets? We are now going back on the return journey."

"Certainly," and realising that our tickets were a single fare, we both purchased another ticket each, telling him that we had not noticed a signpost telling us that this was indeed Pye Corner.

Both of us tried hard to convince him that we were not trying to get a bus ride for nothing, as this certainly looked as if this was the case. We both pointed to where there should be a bus stop sign, telling passengers that this was the end of their journey.

It was difficult to understand the driver with his broken English accent, but it seemed that there was no bus-stop sign, for the vandals kept taking it, or pushing it over.

Arriving back at Speightstown, we decided to have a spot of lunch, and a beer, finding an eating place that was upstairs, on a balcony with the sea just ten feet below us, with the water so clear that you could see the bottom some twenty feet below.

This was the first time that I had seen a kingfish; they are like miniature crocodiles, with mouth and jaws as long as the rest of its body, and here they were, some two feet long, cruising below the surface and what a fine fish they turned out to be.

Days to come, barbied, grilled, fried, boiled, you name it! However, it was cooked it was super. I daresay it is a predator like out pike back home. I suppose when it's their turn for supper, they did not have far to go for their meal, shoals of smaller fry were swimming quite happily farther down in the depths.

Even here, the peaceful and tranquil prevailing conditions made this meal seem as if world-wide problems were non-existent, as it seemed time had stood still. To me it was as if I had shouted to break the silence, the whole of Speightstown would have condemned me.

Arriving back at Bridgetown, I told Martin that I had found it best to purchase a few supplies and make them up before I go to cricket, then take them with me.

"That's a good idea, but I think I will purchase something in the grounds," he said.

We both went into the nearest supermarket. I looked at some rolls, and decided to buy a dozen of them and cheese and a tub of butter and we both purchased large bottles of coke. One I had in mind for diluting later with the rum bottle.

Another welcome party for our new arrivals at the Old Fort, and at six-thirty p.m. some fifty or more of the Mike Burton group were in attendance. With the freebies that were on offer, and the bottle of rum shared between Jennie and Bill, David and Gerald, John and Liz, Martin and myself, plus the two litres of coke, we all had a very pleasant evening. This time cricket was not the only conversation piece, and this I was to find out many times, if there was a subject that seemed interesting, and worthy of discussion, then this was certainly time for an exchange of views.

As holiday bedtimes go, this would have been one of the earlier ones, for everyone was now keen to prepare for an early call for the match tomorrow.

"See you tomorrow."

Day 17 - First day of 4th Test Match

I'm sure the Jenny Wren acts like a clock to my senses, as I was up and walking along the beach at six a.m. This morning was going to be the first of a regular routine I was going to adopt. Just off the edge of the shoreline there was a section of conifers that ran parallel with the high wire fence enclosing the garrison, and here I met up and spoke to a local Barbadian reading his newspaper. We started talking, and told him I was over here supporting the

England cricketers, friendly banter continued for some ten minutes, me finally asking him would he be attending the cricket, and would he be here tomorrow?

He replied, "No, I will be watching it on the box, and yes, I will see you in the morning." I continued walking up through the pine, spruce, cedar trees along the road to the garrison, then down the hill past the entrance, then turning left to the road that led back to the hotel and the Pebbles Restaurant.

This morning I had my breakfast, then went back to the hotel room, to find Martin was ready for the off. I collected my food packs, placing them in my old faithful – a Sainsbury's carrier bag! We both left our keys at the desk, and joined the rest of the group on the coach.

I was seated with the early party in the Sir Gary Sobers Stand, though it seemed a lot of the others were scattered around, Martin included. He was in the stand directly opposite us and had a steel band for company too.

West Indies won the toss and put us into bat. The weather was very warm and it appeared from some of the more knowledgeable amongst us that the decision to field first was mighty unusual for they had a good batting line-up, and the wicket would be suitable for their big guns.

By the lunch-break, both Atherton and Stewart were making this evaluation look a bit ridiculous, as both "were playing out of their skins".

I thought I would go out of the ground to eat my lunch, as quite a number were doing the same. I walked along the pavement and, seeing a couple sitting in a shady doorway with an empty deckchair beside them, enquired, "Could I come in and sit on your spare chair, eat my cheese rolls and drink my beers?"

"Yes, certainly you are most welcome," came the reply, as they introduced themselves as Eddy Codrington and Joyce Bowen. Eddy who was just visiting, was going back to Holders Green later in the day. I did not even ask Eddy which direction or where it might be, for I was having difficulty in understanding him as it was. Joyce, it appeared, was looking after the house and property while the owners were away on holiday.

Eddy asked me, "Do you know how many times England have beaten the West Indies here in Bridgetown?"

I replied, "I have not got a clue."

"Only once before, and then our boys did not have a very strong side out, but this time we mean business."

When I told him, "You will have to start taking some wickets then," this closed the subject down for the time being.

Joyce asked me what part of England I came from. When I said, "Just outside London, in a county called Essex," this cheered her up no end for she said, "I used to live in South London, at Peckham, do you know it?"

When I said I had heard of it, but it was a long way from where I lived, she then told me that she had decided to come back home to pass the rest of her days here, and, God willing, for a long time.

I must say they were both very interesting islanders, and while I was talking to them, Joyce became more and more engaging, especially with her pastimes and hobbies, over the days to come.

England by stumps had scored 299 for 5 wickets. Both the batsman at the time, Graham Hick, 25 no. and Jack Russell 3 no. had been asked if they wanted to bat on in failing light. Both decided to come off. In my own mind at the time, I reflected back to the Port of Spain conditions. Why didn't the umpires have a bit of sympathy then, and offer the choice too, even to those middle-order ones?!

Of this fine innings, Atherton and Stewart had put on an opening stand of 171, Stewart 118 and Atherton 85.

All agreed back on the coach to the hotel that both had laid the foundations for a really big first innings.

Again there was the same voice I overheard at Trinidad, "You don't want to worry, if our boys can score a lot of runs on a docile track, what do you think Richardson, Haynes and company will do. Another voice says, "Wait till Curtly and Courtney get going again!

I told Martin, after I was introduced to his pals he had been sitting with all day, Phil, Alan and Ken, "I am not going far tonight as my legs were playing up a bit. I also want to find out from Julie if she had been able to do anything about my dollars." Seeing her briefly later she told me that she had not had any luck, but will try the next day.

Day 18 - 2nd day of 4th Test Match

Same time, same place—Rudolf (that was his name) was sitting reading his newspaper and as soon as he saw me coming he put his paper up to cover his face, from behind which he said, "I am not talking to you, man," but his good fellowship was quickly back on track. Lifting the sheets away, he uncovered a beaming visage with a smile from ear to ear.

"What sort of witch doctors do you use?" he asked.

"When our boys get going, we do not need any help from anyone," I replied.

He then did admit, "You certainly had the best of yesterday's play."

He tells me he is a coconut collector and seller. I told him about one I had purchased in the Port of Spain and did not like it at all as it did not have any flavour.

"There are a lot of people who sell coconuts who do not know which are the right ones to take from the tree and cannot tell the prime ones from the secondary ones, they are all the same to them."

I told him, "The one I tried had a bitter taste and looked more like water than milk."

"It was not ripe," he said. "When I pick them I make sure they are top quality ones, each and every one—and delicious milk."

"You are a bit old for climbing a ladder, aren't you?" I inquired.

At this, I could see the prickles rising from around his collar and his face just a shade paler than the one I had first approached.

"I am seventy-one and I climb the trees and do not use a ladder of any description." And with this statement I could not only feel how proud Rudolf was of his agility and athleticism in climbing the coconut trees, but I could also feel his indignity at me for thinking along the lines that a ladder had to be used to harvest the coconuts.

As I have always admired older people who just will not give in and say, "That's my lot" on reaching retirement age, I held my hand out and gave his a good shake saying, "Well done."

"I am always selling my coconuts outside St Michael's Church and the trees I pick them from are from a private estate in a small village near St Johns. If they're not ready to be picked they stop there until they are."

I had no reason to doubt Rudolf's word, as he seemed to be a tiny grey-haired man, very lithe-looking and quite capable of climbing the highest tree.

I said, "Time to go—see you tomorrow and may we score a lot more runs."

"Best of luck to you all and may you all be out by the first break," his reply.

At Pebbles Restaurant, Dulcie's guvnor had arrived, the owner himself. I introduced myself and asked him when it was possible for him to allow Dulcie time off to show me part of the island.

"I am sorry," he says, "we have five important days coming up when we have a lot of reserved bookings, people who have paid large deposits and I have to get extra staff in to assist the regulars I employ here now. No there is no way I can let Dulcie have any time off, I am sorry. Are you here to watch the cricket?"

"Indeed I am and we have come to turn your side over!" I replied.

"There is not much fear of that happening—it is just a question of how many runs you will need to avoid an innings defeat."

The weather today gave us blue skies, just the odd one or two clouds that gave us an excellent day's cricket, Hick out in the very first over and England all out for 355.

There was an incident concerning Phil Tufnell during the play mid-morning, but as the press at the time gave it a lot of coverage I don't think it's necessary for me to add any further details. At the close West Indies were 188 for 7, and I'm sure if it had not been for a good recovery from

Curtly Ambrose 30 not out and Chanderpaul 40 not out, putting on an unbroken 54 partnership for the eighth wicket, beating a record set back in 1947 by R Christani and W Ferguson, West Indies would have been long gone and perhaps now following on.

My midday break with Joyce had again been an enjoyable one as she was telling me quite a lot of alterations had been done here in Bridgetown while she had been away in England. I asked her, "Have you regretted leaving here for England in the first place?"

"No, none at all, my education was much improved while I was in you country. In fact the life of the English was very similar to our own lives here in Barbados, a lot of very rich people and a lot of poor ones too. The very poor did not seem to want to better themselves, just accepting what life had brought to them and expecting nothing different."

While I was talking to her, now and the subsequent days, she hardly ever stopped working on the items she was turning out—be it woolly hats of all shapes and sizes, or table mats made from nylon, cotton, coconut fibres or any material she found, she would work so that her nimble fingers would turn whatever it was into an object of beauty. That second day in her company she let me have a look at some of her creative products. I told her then, "It would have put a weaver's wheel to shame. They are magnificent!" I then remarked, "I notice you don't have a pattern book close by, Joyce."

"No, man, my pattern book is up here," touching her forehead.

I said to her about the one she was working on, a table mat of exceptional colouring made of nylon, "It's fit for the

Queen's table," and she had a good laugh at this saying, "It might do in the kitchen."

Back at the hotel everyone was in high spirits, for the day's honours had been shared. I told Martin that I was going for a dip in the pool and I'd see him later.

I don't know how other people felt, but I was glad to get rid of the smells of barbied, roasted, grilled and burnt chicken that stayed with you all day long. Those various methods were used on that poor fowl, so maltreated and abused–in one case I witnessed one being burnt almost to a cinder, and, if you please, placed on a large dish and dressed round with a girdle of fried burnt onions.

During the evening I searched out Julie, who had now been able to get my Trinadadian dollars changed for Barbadian currency.

I did not stop up too late, as for once I had a contented mind to lay on the pillows so I was soon in the land of nod.

Day 19 - 3rd of 4th Test

On my walk-round up past the garrison and Savannah, I could not see Rudolf anywhere. It might have been that he was selling coconuts near St Michael's Church; they would have been ones that he picked yesterday and today was Sunday, so no doubt with the congregation in attendance, trade was excellent. There were also plenty of others who worked on the Sabbath. As I had ambled along the beach two stall-holders who sell beach wear had already put up their stalls–both were huge! (Not the stalls!)–and asked them when I passed by, "What is the weather going to be like today?"

"It's going to be hot, man, and your fielders are going to chase that ball all day long."

Each morning so far, I had been able to get my banner up in some decent position, and with a bit of luck this morning might do the same. As soon as I arrived at the ground, I rushed for the spot as two young banner proprietors were aiming for the same position that I had in mind, but fortunately there was room for each one and no more space. We all agreed that if they did not see our banners where they were placed back home, they must be blind.

The West Indies went on to make 304, their last three wickets adding 170 runs with Curly Ambrose making 44 and Chanderpaul 77, he took over five hours to make those runs before he was caught by Ramprakash bowled Tufnell, this the only wicket he took in the innings. Fraser's final figures of 28-5.5.7.75.8 were the best figures he has had for his country. England at the close of play had scored 171 for 3 wickets, Atherton, Smith and Ramprakash were out. Nearly 100 runs Hick and Stewart have put on and England now with a lead of 222 runs, still 7 wickets to fall. Most of us on the coach back to the hotel were in a good mood believing in only one outcome. I somehow came back with supporters from another tour group, and I was mighty glad to depart from their company. I know at the time I thought that if I had been involved in their company from the outset I would have gone back home. Bed at eleven-forty-five.

Day 20 - Rest day from Cricket

I was up and about just after six-thirty this morning so I took a longer walk, this time right round the Savannah and then had breakfast at the Pebbles. John, Liz and Telly Kelly had now gone back home and had promised to keep an eye open for my banner.

Back in Room 311 Martin says he is getting, like me, short of dollars, so we get Key 46 for our safe deposit box to replenish our pockets. I told him that I was going to visit a zoo today so I would see him later, but I wanted to have a dip first.

When I arrived at the beach I expected it to be quite busy—not so, it was Monday, everyone back to work and only seven altogether of which I was one.

I was looking forward to the Barbados Zoo, as when I had seen the advert, it also said you could view Oughterson House and look at its valuable antiques. The zoo had a fine collection of exotic birds.

Taxi-bus down to Bridgetown, then a bus connection to Marley Vale, then another one to the Barbados Zoo.

It was a very pleasant ride through sugar-cane country. In places, both sides of the highway had been fired to burn the stubble and preparations for new crops were well underway. Only a couple of passengers were on board the bus, but though I tried to chat to them it appeared from their looks that they could not understand me! As I very well know, this is not unusual at all.

I had already told the driver that I wanted to get off near the zoo. Shortly after we had passed a sign saying "The Zoo" he called out, "The zoo, man."

There was no sign as to what direction I was supposed to take. Nearby I saw a tractor driver in the fields and going across to him just as he was completing the headlands, I asked him where the zoo might be. Pointing in the opposite direction to the one I was going he said, "That way."

I think I must have walked half a mile, so I paid my entrance fee of two dollars and went straight to the cafe and purchased two ice-cool beers (Banks), all the time seeing what was going on. Not a lot: with the temperature between thirty-five and forty degrees, all the wise humans, animals and birds were doing the right thing– keeping in the shade, or, like me, having a cold drink.

A chap from outside spotted me all alone drinking, so came in to tell me he was the owner of both house and zoo and had I come to view the antiques, to purchase or to view? I told him neither, but I would like to have a look round if I may. "Yes by all means," he said, guiding me to the very impressive oak-panelled door, then saying to me, "Each year I have one, my birthday's today." Before I looked round, would I join him and his wife on the terrace to drink his health?

"Most certainly," I replied.

I had a good walk around, discovering that Oughterson House had indeed some rather memorable pieces. Again, it was a property that was supported by the National Trust. There was only a handful of people there and you could gather from the conversation, and from what you saw that plenty of dollars were needed–not only to keep the place open, but for a whole lot of improvements that had been planned and approved.

I did not offer my NT card but when I left I put a few extra dollars in the "please help" box.

I suppose I was a bit disappointed with the zoo in general. When I began exploring the grounds the macaws, parrots, parakeets, et cetera offered at each cage you passed a colour display that I admit I had not seen bettered anywhere. But this was about the only plus. I followed a botanical trail that led me through a wooded section. Here there was no chance of seeing a specific type of tree, for there were so many of the various species that each was struggling for survival due to overcrowding.

Most of the animals I saw that were native to the island looked the worse for wear, no doubt because of the very hot conditions prevailing.

Back at the house and veranda, the family now had several more guests so I joined them in a final drink. There was only one person present who seemed interested in cricket, and when he realised that I was one of the English supporters asked me, "Why is it when England get in a good position we generally slip up? Either the batting lets us down when we are chasing runs to win, or else the bowlers do not keep a good line or length, isn't that correct?"

I replied by saying that I had only seen one test match and that was only last week for real, so "I could not agree more! This time, though, we have got a good chance of pulling this off."

"Well all of us here are English and of course we want the old country to win, but it seems most unlikely when there is another West Indies innings to come. Anyhow, best of luck."

It was almost two p.m. so I thanked them, wishing them well with their programmes. The owners said to me, "We shall look forward to seeing you next time around."

I walked back to the bus stop on the main road and looked at it carefully, making sure that indeed there was no timetable at all. The driver had told me that they run every half an hour, so I waited for twenty minutes. Giving up, I decided to stretch my legs so I started down the road we had come up on, thinking if a bus came along I would thumb a lift. I had walked a fair distance when I came across a banana plantation on my right-hand side. I would not have known if I had not seen the bananas growing on them. I thought I would pop in and find a nice ripe one, but two women came out, the younger one came straight up to me and asked what I wanted. I told them I was looking for a ripe banana.

"There is only green ones, all the ripe ones have gone to market."

I said, "Do you think I could take a photo of you with some of the banana trees?"

While I was doing this, the other lady called out, "Show him right round, Bessie."

I told Bessie that I was from England and was walking to catch a bus back to Bridgetown, how often did they run and was I going in the right direction?

She said there was a bus stop just a little way down the road.

As we walked further down, I saw indeed that they were all green and not one ripe one. I asked her "How many trees are there?"

Her reply: "There are several fields, must be thousands."

Back to the entrance I said, "Cheerio, I don't want to miss my bus."

They had told me that one was due in less than ten minutes.

Back on the road, I continued walking in the direction that the girls had told me, when a car stopped. It was the birthday chap who said, "Jump in!"

I told him that I was mighty surprised to see him, as I thought he was entertaining his guests.

"The wife wants some more bread from the shop further into the village, so I'll drop you off at the next junction. I know there is a bus-stop sign just along the road on the left."

A couple of minutes later, we arrived at the junction and there, sure thing, the bus sign. I thanked the birthday man and made my way to the stop. Once again—what I had come to expect—there was nothing on it that would inform me of any times or where it was going, or, for that matter, whether it ran at all.

I was keeping my eyes open for now there were three roads that might bring a bus to me, but it must have been an half an hour before a bus came towards me going in the same direction I had just come along. It was travelling empty—no number or destination back or front. Another good ten minutes when, lo and behold, a bus came along heading in the direction of Bridgetown and stopped right beside me.

I asked the driver, "Where is this one going to?"

"Bridgetown," the driver said, "but you are sure is a lucky man. I saw you waiting here a while back and guessed that you wanted to get back to town. We don't come this way on a Monday so you can count your blessings that in me you have found a knight in shining armour."

I thanked him telling him, "This is a funny way to run a bus service. Where do you normally go then?"

"We go straight on." He pointed in the same direction that the birthday man had gone, then shrugging his shoulders he released the brakes saying, "We'll soon have you back in Bridgetown."

Just after five p.m. we arrived back at the terminal. Thanking the driver, I made my way to a taxi-bus. Back in my room I found my swimming trunks and towel and went straight into the sea. By now, my knee was playing up and giving me quite a lot of concern, I suppose in retrospect it was because of how I have mistreated it today. Early night in bed at eleven.

Day 2l - 4th day of 4th Test

Six a.m. It was a beautiful morning again—no clouds as I walked along the beach. Every day I had noticed a flower like our sweet pea at home, but this one was like a convolvulus with long pods already ripened, full of seed, not unlike a runner bean. It was creeping everywhere and as I moved further up the beach it became more dense and concentrated, with, to my surprise, plenty of bean foliage and purple flowers, but no seed pods. This was some way from the shoreline. Why this was I could not fathom a guess, for every part of the beach had the same amount of light and sun as any other part. No doubt nature knew the answer! Continuing on my morning constitutional, for I had not seen Rudolf on my way up and round past the garrison. What did catch my eye was the amount of No 11 buses.

After my breakfast I walked back partway along the beach, then crossed back to walk up the main drive to the hotel. As always about this time, there are three (very well proportioned) Barbadian women, sweeping and generally making the place look respectable again after the night before. There were only two this morning and each day so far there had been some friendly banter between us.

I called out as I was passing, "Did you see that snake?"

"Why, man, that was our witch doctor telling us you am doing a good job."

"Who are your employers and why can't they find you some better tools to work with?" I asked.

"Why, man,"—now lots of laughter—"we are going too fast now, you leave this job to us and go and cheer your cricket team, they are the ones that want to move more quickly...and give them a wider bat as well."

This remark had the other larger lady hanging onto her broom handle to stop her falling over (can you imagine that twenty-stone plus with the beam-end shaking all about?). "Oh dear, Oh dear," came the cry and of course other English cricket supporters were having a good laugh as well. Walking off, I called out, "You wait and see."

The coach left at eight-thirty-five. Again, I had made up a nice lot of rolls for my breaks, all carried in my faithful carrier bag. I had noticed when we were here on Sunday that If I could reach a certain place near to where the players come out from the pavilion, it would be a super spot for my banner. I just beat another two lads who were bent on the same mission. We had a little chat, them asking me how long was I stopping for. All day was my reply. In fact, I had come two-thirds round the ground to get this advantageous position, I stayed for a while and then went in search of my seat. When play started Graham Hick had a job to get started, spending nearly three-quarters of an hour to score another 7 runs; then he was out for 59. Most of the knowledgeable ones said there was no need for a go-slow, as it was a good batting track.

I just listened thinking he was doing his job keeping an end up.

At the close of play with undoubtedly England taking the honours, having declared at 394 for 7 wickets, Alec Stewart scoring 143 and Graham Thorpe 84, to plenty of green ones like myself this looked a formidable target for the West Indies of 446 to win. Already they had lost two wickets in scoring 47 runs, and with both Richardson and Haynes carrying injuries, what was tomorrow going to bring?

On the coach back to the hotel, most agree that if Lara gets motoring this impossible total could be reached. The knowledgeable ones maintained very few teams batting last had scored runs of this quantity; another said, "A couple of countries have won scoring over 400 runs." Back in our room Martin does look rough and tells me that he is sure it's a pie he has eaten in the ground. We had arranged to go to a cocktail party later, but Martin says, "I am going to give it a miss, see you tomorrow."

The usual group I had palled up with were all in high spirits again as it seemed only rain would save them, the West Indies, from defeat. It was quite late when I took the lift up.

Day 22 - 5th and final day of 4th test

I told Martin that I would see him down at the ground later, after he had told me he was not all up to scratch, but would not miss the last day by any means. My problems were with my knee and this morning seemed extra bad, for I was having a job to bend it. I had decided to walk up to the clinic, which was near the Savannah— they might be able to give me some painkillers.

Arriving at eight-fifty a.m. and as I was a visitor and had not made an appointment, I would have to wait until all the patients had been seen. At ten-ten a nurse came and took me through to see the doctor on duty, who asked me, "Are you one of the England cricket supporters?" She then told me that she was from England, now living here permanently and would not go back to be part of all the rush and madness that goes on there. "What's the trouble?"

I told her as I had tried to explain to the nurse, that I had had an arithroscopy operation some eighteen months ago and found that if I did too much to my legs, both became quite painful. She said, "I think an injection and a few pills would do the trick." She then left the nurse to look after me. She promptly did the business with a good jab in my butt with Volterol, also giving me three tablets a day for a week. Saying, "You will soon be better," with a super smile she handed me the bill for thirty dollars.

Catching a taxi-bus down to Bridgetown I walked round to the taxi ranks, as play had already started and, though it was not far, I did not want to miss any more of the play.

Here waiting for a taxi too were the three lads from Wales. I said, "Are you going to the ground, if so could I join you and share the expense?"

"Yes by all means."

They were soon all aboard with their banner as well. This one had Usk C.C. and with a magnificent dragon painted in red and green. The driver started up, drew away from the kerb, abruptly stopped and said, "We have a puncture—that's torn it."

I said to the lads as we all piled out, "Do you want me to stay with you boys as I seem to be a gremlin to most people?"

The answer from them all, "No you stay with us, come on let's grab another taxi."

Arriving some ten minutes later at the ground, we saw what we all dreaded—LARA there and still batting, the time eleven-fifteen a.m., and him looking as if he was going to stay all day. In fact the voice that had become familiar to me said, as I passed to claim my seat, "He is going to be there all day, you mark my word."

Phil Tufnell was bowling at one end and delivering balls of such accuracy that he stayed at one end for most of the West Indies innings. At the other end Caddick, Fraser and Lewis were doing the business, and making it difficult for the batters to score, with every now and again a wicket going down. When Lara was out, caught by Tufnell at deep mid-wicket, and then Chanderpaul, out just before the lunch interval, it seemed as if an upset was now highly probable.

At this time in the match, the noise around the ground was deafening. Where Martin and the rest of the England supporters were, steel bands in this particular stand were at times equalled by the English contingent, but of course throats had to become second-best as the morning session came to an end.

I made my way down the steps and out of the ground before the main stampede started, walking just the short distance to Joyce's house. And, seeing the door open, I knew that I was welcome. As usual she was busy doing her artistry with the various needles, this time she had almost completed a beret, again one of many colours.

I said to her, "Is it all right to have my cheese rolls and beers?"

"Why, of course, man, you know you are most welcome. What do you think of the colour mix in this one I've almost completed?"

I thought I might as well do a deal here with Joyce, as they seemed worthwhile pressies to take home.

I asked her, "Have you got many of the ones with the coloured rings round?"

"Why I sure have, man." This then started a search in a big chest full of all manner of articles, so after I had completed my meal and finished my beers we started doing business. We discussed each item and its value; quite often my habit on these occasions is to haggle over the prices but each time an item was put in front of me and a price suggested I looked round the sparsely furnished room, with its lino-covered floor well worn in places and the concrete showing through in both rooms. This time I just could not enter into this kind of purchase, though I reasoned that Joyce was not necessarily near the breadline, but maybe mighty close. I was pretty sure she relied on some of these woollen, nylon, coconut and cotton masterpieces to help fund her meagre income.

I asked her, "How long have you been retired?"

She either did not understand or did not want to, for now she had found an even bigger chest with more hats and berets, plus jumpers all made of the same materials.

Eventually when my purchases had reached twenty-five dollars, I then gave her thirty. Over the moon was not the word, for she flung her arms round my neck saying, "When are you coming back to Barbados, man?"

I said, "I doubt if I would come back again, but if I do I will look you up," thanking her very much for letting me stop and have my lunch with her.

Back at the ground, everybody was in celebratory mood, very confident of things to come. An announcement about two-thirty—would all supporters of both the West Indies and England please keep off the pitch. This was going to be impossible to keep to for the din around us was really deafening.

Just before three, Chris Lewis sent Curtly Ambrose's stumps flying, the West Indies out for 237, so England had won by 208 runs.

The whole field was covered with followers of the teams in less than two minutes of this wicket falling and I don't mind telling you that I was one of the hundreds who invaded. What was nice was that for once all the noise was coming from the English contingent, those fans who had Union Jacks—even the Welsh Dragons were all getting in on the act. What I was sure about was that the steel drums of the Barbadians had quietly been made to take a back seat.

Phil Tufnell's contribution of 36 overs, 12 maidens, 100 runs and 3 wickets together with Andy Caddick's 17 overs, 3 maidens, 65 runs and 5 wickets were a credit to them both. Both Geoff Lewis and Angus Fraser backed them up; I know it was hot under the roof of the stand, but guessing what it was like chasing the ball about in the middle, it must have been well worth it for it was a mighty happy lot of England cricketers who were applauded all the way to the pavilion. And this was the best of it—there were still 29 overs left to bowl. Evidently it was the first win at this ground since 1934-35, fifty-nine years ago, so really this victory was long overdue.

I collected my banner and was now like a lot of other banner-bearers letting the team know that we had all come a long way and had waited a long time for this result. I was not surprised to find home loyalists were coming up to me and shaking my hand, most saying, "The best team won, man." Of course, I, like my comrades-in-arms was giving our banners the treatment: "High Beach and Essex". I had several photographers come up and ask me if they could have a photo of me holding up the banner. One chap did ask me, "Where's that in England?" He turned out to be a local Barbadian after we had had a chat on both teams' performances.

On the coach back to the hotel, I was surprised how quiet it seemed. After talking to a well-seasoned veteran of many tours sitting nearby, he mentioned to me, "So often we have been in a position like the one at Port of Spain, and then they've fallen at the last hurdle. This wants some taking in—today we won well and convincingly."

Back at the happy hour bar, we found as many as sixty-five different drinks were at half price and then when management found out this was very popular, it was extended by, wait for it, five minutes. Martin has been around all the day and tells me he has not enjoyed the day all that much, owing to being under the weather; he says his tummy is now much worse than yesterday. Back in the room by eleven-thirty I made up my diary and am sure I went straight off.

Day 23

Six-fifteen a.m. walk along the beach, Rudolf the coconut man sees me coming and offers his hand, saying, "You was the better team, man, and deserved to win."

We soon got back into a conversation, for I realised that if I wanted to pick more of Rudolf's brain I would have to hurry for we were going on tomorrow. I, by this time, wanted to know more about the coconut trees. I had with me my notebook and told him straightaway that I intended to jot down some of his knowledge. For a good ten minutes I stood there putting down some interesting features. I, and anybody else, would have been very much astounded, dumbfounded and amazed to discover it had so many rewarding gifts.

"The coconut tree grows for up eighty years and provides up to 100 coconuts from each one each season. I start selling them when the tree is seven to eight years of age, its age dated from when the seed has germinated."

I asked him, "When they fall from the tree, why don't they split?"

"Because the fibre round the shell stops it from smashing, it acts like a cushion. I regularly see them fall from up to 100 feet. The fibre is very important to everyone on the island–sails, rope, paper, nets, mats, quilts, hats, brushes of all kinds, artists, boot, brooms or paint. You and me, our families, we could live on what it supplies–for our clothing and for the home we dwell in, from the coconut comes oil, candles, margarine, oil for lubricating machinery and soap. That's just a few of the products from our coconut tree."

He said this with a convincing smile. I know I managed to jot down most of what Rudolf passed on, but could have missed several items. He had spoken quite clearly in his Pigeon English, I know I said to him, "It's remarkable how many goods are produced from something that I only thought you got milk from."

He then asked me, "Here is a question for you–why do all the coconut trees lean towards the sea or the ocean?"

I answered, "No, I have not got a clue and to tell you the truth I had never noticed this."

On this occasion, he let me down when he said, "I thought you might have told me that."

I told him I had enjoyed talking to him and thanked him for passing on some of his wisdom to me, shaking his hand.

"When are you going back to England?" he asked.

My reply: "When we have beaten you in Antigua, then we go home."

"Why, man, you have no fear of that. Your witch doctors helped you here, but not in St Johns. We have some mighty fine ones who live nearby in the east. In fact right near the cricket ground."

I considered after I continued walking what he had meant by his last remark? I do know that I am much more knowledgeable as a result of the various topics of conversation we had engaged in over recent days, and was pleased to have given him some of my building trade education and a few helpful suggestions for his problems.

All my limbs seem to be heaps better, as I walked on round to Pebbles Restaurant for the last time, as we were off in the afternoon.

A new assistant is serving us this morning, Tina, who says to me, "Are you Percy?"

I said, "Yes."

"Dulcie the other girl did so much want to drive you round the island."

And when she asked whether I will be back I said, "I doubt if I shall come this way again."

Back in the hotel, Martin is still well under the weather, but has phoned the doctor who has suggested that he sees the nurse in the hotel as there is always one on duty for emergencies like this.

I finish packing and take my case down for departure and see Phil, Ken and Alan, all of us agreeing that Martin is giving us all reasons for concern.

One-thirty, the coach arrives to take us to the Grantly Adams Airport. Martin does not seem to have improved at all, and of course the delay of three hours before the plane leaves is not helping him, or, come to that, any of us. Fortunately, I had now acclimatised to the extreme weather conditions that enveloped us here.

One thing I did notice at this airport was that very large groups went through Departures very quickly, because their passports had already been collected and they all went through en-bloc—of course then they were in Departures first with the best seats.

Four-forty-five—up and away, the flight took just forty minutes, yet by the time we had gone through the usual procedures it was dark when we reached our hotel. I did notice, on coming to the entrance, that we passed what looked like sentry boxes and could not quite fathom out the lay-out of the St James Club, which was to be our final abode for the duration of our tour.

The time was now seven-thirty. On our arrival complications was not the word for the situation most of us found ourselves in. Quickly, a softening-up approach by way of drinks was offered to those of us who had no room for the night. No doubt this was a nice gesture but not enough when many tired travellers were almost out on their feet. Added to this, if you wanted to have some air you had to climb up and down a dozen steps.

We quickly heard that the hotel had been overbooked. This would not have been so bad and normally would have been resolved quite quickly, but unfortunately looking at the maps of the hotel and its position, the nearest one would be miles away. We just had to be patient.

Julie and Roseanne, our tour managers, were doing everything to pacify and console a lot of disgruntled supporters. All of us had been given more drinks to keep the situation from overheating. Eventually Barry from Devon, Phil from Bristol, Martin and yours truly agreed to room-share when the management asked if we would like to share an annex apartment, which was a fair distance from the main part of the hotel. "Yes, of course," we all said.

So, sorting out our luggage, which was then placed on board an electric buggy, very similar to the ones you see buzzing round golf courses, but this being the difference: it held four people quite comfortably plus the driver. It was now past ten p.m.

Dark, very narrow roads, only eight feet wide—this I might be exaggerating! S-bends led us to our destination. I immediately thought about a television series called *The Prisoner*—the little narrow roads and buggies that featured in the series fitted the present situation perfectly. We pulled up with roofs on one side and front doors on the other. The driver says, "Phone number 19 from the telephone inside the flat and a buggy would be dispatched straightaway to pick you up."

Up at the main part of the hotel, bars and casinos are open sixteen hours of every day, so down the winding steps we all went at speed, and here, for a start, I must compliment the architect for the eight-foot wide stone steps, twenty in number, that led us to the front door of No 429.

On entering we were all taken aback by the size of the place, two huge bedrooms with en-suite facilities, a dining room you could have put the whole of my ground floor at home in and plenty of space over, an adjoining open-plan kitchen with every modern convenience attached with a superb worktop that served as a table for maybe six people or more. What a place, we all agreed! I had gone to the curtains and pulled them to one side, which uncovered a lattice type of blind screening the huge French windows. Peeping through, I said, "Have a look at that." We all agreed it was a nice patio leading to some steps, which in turn led onto a nice lawn.

Barry from Devon says, "I'll be the first there in the morning." I said, "Don't you sweat on that!"

Everybody had had a quick wash and change that made us all look a lot more presentable, when the buggy arrived in answer to our request on line 19. Up at headquarters nobody stopped long as we were all knackered and Martin had not come with us. When we got back we asked him how he was feeling, to this his reply was: "Still the same."

I wrote up my diary and got into bed—not quite a king-size one but big enough—and was quickly asleep I'm sure.

Day 24

A long narrow window was opposite my bed and as daylight began, I could see a shaft of sunlight cutting a swathe across the lino-covered floor. Time to get up—quickly slipping into my shorts I walked to the French windows and, hardly making a sound, I drew back the curtains and slid the shutters up. Looking through the glass, I could hardly believe my eyes. I drew a deep breath and slightly opened the sliding door just enough for me to squeeze through, I pinched myself saying quietly to myself (being afraid to waken my room mates), "This must be mighty near to paradise."

The scene I was gazing on had to be seen to be believed, for what we all thought last night was a lawn was sand that runs right round the bay as far as the eye can see. Standing on the top of the few steps–"WOW!" There, not a cricket pitch away, was the very silent, tranquil, peaceful and welcoming Atlantic Ocean. I just stood taking in as much of this delight trying to understand why there was not even a ripple of water on the surface, whatever direction took my eye. Now as my gaze took in the things immediately around me, I noticed on one side of the patio a palm tree and on the other a bougainvillaea full of purple blossom.

I crept stealthily back inside and searched out the linen cupboard, which was packed with towels and sheets. Selecting a huge bath towel I retraced my steps tiptoeing out of the chalet down the steps and in the water in a brace of shakes, the temperature of the water from this very first visit never seemed to change, lukewarm, tepid, no even warmer than that. You had to go a fair distance from the shore to get out of your depth and even then I found that the change of depth made no difference to your body heat, and whatever part of this inlet you were swimming in the buoyancy was the same. I am sure if I had tried that I could have floated from one side to the other. How far?–As close to a mile as makes no difference.

I saw a person walking past and asked her, "What is the time, please?" Six-thirty came the reply, so I carried on, I reckoned, for another half an hour, just floating and just thinking that I must have done something special or a good deed, either accidentally or purposely to be rewarded like this. I knew something straightaway–this morning and all subsequent ones, while we are staying here, this is going to be my routine.

Arriving back at the steps to the chalet, there was Barry who called out to me, "Have you got the key to the French windows?"

As he reached me I said, "No, I left them open."

To my reply he said, "I saw them open so I locked them up and went out through the front door and up the steps."

"Well where is the key to the front door?" I asked.

He then said, "It must still be in the apartment if you haven't got it."

I scratched my head and wondered, so I said, "We are locked out."

"Seems like it," and he then walked off.

Between the chalets there was a pretty tight passage. This was filled with small stones, quite a number of them were like walking over sharp pieces of flint. Barry by this time had come back and had realised too that we were locked out, so he joined me. Like me he was bare-footed, so this short walk was mighty painful to say the least. After another discussion we walked round the back again and banged on Phil's bedroom window to let him know that we are locked out and after a bit of noise he draws the curtains. He then proceeds to the French windows and opens them up saying, "What are you doing this time of the morning?" Martin is also awake and wants to know what is going on. The time now is seven-forty-five.

I guessed from this first experience that we were going to have some fun and games here.

Looking at a map of the St James Club Complex, which was placed very handy on a board on the opposite side of the road at the top of our steps, I saw that the provision shop was several levels and properties higher. All the roads took you up or down, but there was also a short cut (I should have counted them!) up several hundred steps. So, as you now realise, this place originally had been, before development, a fairly large and steep hillside. Seeing a person walking past we asked him if he knew what time the shop opened, for, as you can gather, our cupboard was bare. "Eight," came the reply.

I made my way by the road route, a surprisingly long way. I made some purchases, tea, coffee, milk and sugar. I bought only bread and butter for myself as it looked like toast was going to be a favourite here, I quickly found out that this was the one shop so it was extremely expensive—nothing you can do about it as you have to eat and drink.

At nine we phone for a buggy to take us up to breakfast—you either paid for it, put it on your tab or booked it to your room. Martin is not coming—now he has more flat-mates they can see that he is indeed suffering from that dreaded tummy bug.

Cricket does not start until tomorrow so we can please ourselves what we do today, I had already made up my mind what I was going to do and that was to be in and out of the water most of the day. I found out where more of our group were, now that people were up and about. Dave and Gerald were sharing the same sort of chalet as us. Three lads from Bristol were with them; Phil, Paddy and yet another Phil were on the seashore, just like us, but overlooking us all as they were perched quite high on the very top of a small mountain. 500 feet up we were told there is another chalet. We found out later that Dave and Sylvia, the honeymoon couple, were up there together with a swimming pool. He has had the paper delivered to him, the buggy picks him up and he enjoys the same terms as us. "Can't be bad for the price," he was known to quote on several occasions.

At midday the boys from 435 and the ones in 429 agreed to hold a party in 429's chalet, agreed time seven. I called on "tall Phil"; he had popped in and taken a look round at our kitchen, saying, "Yes, this will do." Each of us had been allocated various ingredients to purchase, I forget how many times I went up and down the steps and was only pleased that my painful limbs were holding up. On delivery of whatever, they were rewarded with a dip in the Atlantic (for at times I had worked up a sweat down the steps) when I would dive into the sea, float and watch the clouds go by. MAGIC!

There is not much to say about our party; we all enjoyed each other's company. I brought out the headware that I had purchased from Joyce back in Barbados. Phil did nearly all the cooking for all nine of us. Mind you, I don't think that Martin ate much, if anything at all. The smell associated with fry-ups is not a healthy pick-me-up for queasy tummies. Very few of the cans were left, rums and cokes, rums and mixes–bottles of several brands were put away, making this quite a memorable night. Tall Phil also acted as the account-ant and Martin, now with a few beers tucked away is acting as his assistant, the price in all a staggering twenty-four dollars each, and we did not have to pay for a taxi. Dave from Northampton did suggest that they have a buggy to take them home, but a committee meeting over-ruled this. A final toast: "To England's next win with the match starting tomorrow." Twelve-fifteen: all the boys from 435 left by way of the seashore. "See you tomorrow."

Day 25 - First day of 5th and final test

This morning I was more determined to walk a good way round and had put my sandals on for any rough country that I might find. I was glad I did because the further I went so there was more and more rubbish—glass, tins, old rusty pieces of iron, and then I had a job to understand what some large lumps of square machinery were. After a good investigation, I realised they were three safes (as fitted in banks) you could see where each one had been jemmied open and by their condition they had been here for a considerable time.

I had come to a point where I had to walk right at the water's edge and the beach, but now the tip (for this was what I had reached) had come right down into the sea. Looking up at the hillside, I noticed about a dozen head of cattle and could see they were making for the way I had come along, so, quickly taking particular notice of one large male who had all his working parts, I decided to turn round and go back.

Martin, I knew before I left, had had a shocking night but when I got back he had decided to come up for breakfast. This time we went in to another restaurant. Overlooking the sea, it was the same sort of food as provided in the main complex, but at half the price.

Just before we get onto the coach, Roseanne tells us that she has had four match tickets stolen from her last night: they are seats sitting near some of us in the Andy Roberts Stand—so keep an eye open for any strangers and let her know straightaway.

Rentford our driver is a Rasterferian and likes to tell us about himself, his long hair and his very large hat. I don't think he stopped talking all the time we were in the taxi-bus. He was excellent company, but he certainly met his match with some of our lads when it came to the cross-banter that at time had the company in fits of laughter.

From whence we started, we had to go across the island to the Recreation Ground at St Johns. This journey was going to be a very memorable one later but, for now, to see the road surface in daylight hours, you wondered how any kind of vehicle passed safely over it. Huge holes–in some cases the size of a double dustbin lid–all had to be safely negotiated this morning and on subsequent ones, Rentford was without doubt pothole-perfect. Many times the co-driver, or those sitting at good vantage points would cry, "There's another one!" Yet during all the excursions we made there and back, not once did we collide with any other transport.

Along the road on either side–just to make the trip all the more unforgettable–were concrete channels. No, these were not your small little six-inch ones, these were four feet wide by four feet deep, and, if you please, along the top edge and directly beside the carriageway, they cleverly disguised a strip of purposely neglected turf, in places flowers in blossom–"Whew!"

As I recall this, I can only remember seeing one car in the giant gully and that had been pushed in. I had seen through the front part of the taxi-bus, from way back in it, several youths pushing it along the road. Then, when we passed, it was down the side and in the water with all the lads waving to us. At the time lots of guesses went round as to what had occurred, one voice suggested, "To push it out of the way." Who could disagree?

Arriving at the ground and alighting from the coach, I

was very surprised to discover how narrow the pavements were—certainly not wide enough for two people to walk along comfortably, especially given that now and again a huge pole of substantial girth and carrying electricity cable took up two-thirds of this space.

Curtly Ambrose was the West Indian Skipper and, nothing unusual, won the toss and decided to take first knock. At 12 runs for 2 wickets a lot of the green ones, myself included, were thinking and saying that they would be all out by the end of the day.

I had placed my banner in a superb spot and had left instructions with the rum-seller nearby to keep an eye on it for me. By the lunch interval the score stood at 48 for the 2 wickets, our bowlers doing what they do best, sometimes bowling tight.

I had already made up my bagels, purchased my beers, obtained my pass-out ticket and was soon walking along the road opposite the ground entrance. As I went further I noticed a garden gate open, a nice patio, some easy chairs beneath a plastic corrugated-roofed lean-to. I knocked on the door of the property and asked the elderly gent who answered it, if I could sit and eat my sustenance there.

"Certainly," came the reply and, guessing right that I was an England Cricket supporter, he asked, "You are English?...And are most welcome." He then introduced himself. "I am George and this is my wife Isabelle," she having now put in an appearance and also offered her hand in friendship.

I made myself at home in a nice comfortable armchair, very different to the ones in the grounds, with George saying, "We will let you eat your food in peace. If there's anything that you need don't be afraid to ask, just let us know."

I should think there was a spy-hole somewhere, as I had hardly finished when George put in an appearance from round the side of the house. He then told me quite a lot about himself; both he and Isabelle had been school teachers, were now retired and had five sons and not one of them interested in cricket. From this chance knock on a stranger's door I could not have realised I would soon learn how a middle-class Antiguian gentleman ticked from day to day.

While I was busy listening to George, I was also taking particular notice of his garden especially the blossoms of a nearby frangipani tree, which was also the home of a large iguana and several smaller ones. The latter were close to me and one was appearing now and then on the top of the three-feet high wall surrounding us, about ten inches in length and as quick as lightning. In this first visit to George's property, I realised that many of the plants and shrubs needed water; they weren't without life, but were as near to it as makes no difference. A couple of orange trees further down the garden with a large number of green fruit had me thinking to myself at the time, here's a case for water.

What did draw my attention was a poinsettia. I said to George as soon as I set my eyes on it, "Is that a wild one?"

"It's been here longer than us so I suppose it is a wild one. Every two or three years we give it a damn good prune to keep its height and width in check, but that's all."

I said to him, "You know, to get the red bracts at home in England we have to make them change colour by keeping the whole plant in semi-darkness for quite a long period, maybe several months, so that they'll change to a deep red."

"No, nobody does anything to them here, they just change naturally. It's not a brilliant red, what you see now is the final colour," George replied. "You have to remember that here in Barbados it is always dusty and this seems to adhere to foliage and bracts." Then looking at his watch he added, "You know, Percy, play has started again."

I said, "Can I pop in and see you tomorrow?"

"Yes of course you are most welcome."

The afternoon play was very similar to the morning session, a good battle between bat and ball but at the close of play the West Indies were certainly in the driving seat, having scored 274 for 3. Lara was 164 not out and Arthurton was keeping his end up in support, Adams had contributed a handy 59.

When I went down to untie my banner from the wire mesh fence the rum-seller and his family were just packing up, so I had a quick rum and told him to keep the change. I presumed it was his daughter who helped me with the banner—"WHEW!"

On the coach back to the St James Club, we all looked not unlike the English fielders—knackered!

It was about nine p.m. and we were all sitting down reading, writing or doing something when we heard a knock on the door. An Antiguian girl came in, telling us she wanted to turn our beds down. She also brought in loads of clean linen, telling us that her brother was Kenneth Benjamin the West Indian cricketer. She seemed a very friendly person, telling us a lot about the island and that she owned a farmhouse in the country district of All Saints and that she only worked here to help pay the bills as she has two children to feed and support. Edith was her name; while we are here she will look after us and "not to worry abut making the beds".

We all gave a big cheer at this news, even Martin who was now well on the way to recovery. She could not understand why we had come all this way to see our team defeated. "Very strange..."

I asked her, "Is there any chance of getting some pieces of sugar cane to take home to England?

"Yes, of course, I'll bring some in tomorrow."

"How about bottles of rum?" I asked.

"How many do you want?" I was a bit taken aback by this, as I only wanted to take a bottle or two home as presents so I said, "Just a couple if you could manage it, many thanks."

After she left, we discussed Edith and how dedicated she appeared to be to her job. If she looks after six of these properties and keeps them wholesome each day that's not a job to look forward to each day. Our own kitchen, we were to find, had the full treatment—cups and saucers, all kitchen utensils nicely put back where they belonged.

Day 26 - Day 2 of Fifth and Final Test

6.30 I was up for a swim and a walk along the beach. Back in the kitchen, we have all sorted out where we store each other's food, etc. It's surprising really because none of us had met any of the others before. Not one of us likes what the other person would eat and drink, not even sugar or milk, the latter for instance, either bottled, canned or dried. In our short time together, you could see each of us had a whim of some description.

Martin this morning nearly missed the transport. We three took the buggy up for the coach, Phil, Barry and myself, with the understanding that Martin would catch a buggy up and join us. The telephone rang at reception to say that Martin was locked in 429 and could not get out. One of us had the key and, quickly handing it over, the culprit said he had not realised. Phil tore down to the chalet and rescued him. We spoke about this when we met up and agreed that, with this particular type of lock and fitting, no way could Martin have got out. Even if he let himself out of the French windows he could still not have locked them as they could only be locked from the inside. We had several laughs about the situation Martin had been placed in later, but, as Martin says, it was not very funny to be locked in a place you can't get out of.

On the coach most of the cricket buffs agreed that Lara could well beat Sir Gary Sobers' Record Test Score of 365 today and just as many say if he is still there at close of play he will certainly reach the target tomorrow. "WHEW!"

What we did agree with was the fact that the poor old England's fielding was going to have a fair old battering, if Lara indeed was still there later today.

The rum-seller had put his stall up already by the time we arrived and, as I could see a better position for my banner, I moved round to fasten it to the wire fencing. While I was doing this I kept my eye open on both sides of the boundary, and had almost finished when a voice said, "Take that down." A policeman had approached me from behind my back, from the Cricket Square.

"Surely, officer, it is doing no harm here," I said.

"I have orders to say that you must not put your flag up here."

It was no good arguing, I had to obey.

I went back to the original place I had put it yesterday and this was where it stayed for the duration of the match.

Only a short distance from our seats in the Andy Roberts Stand, another rum-seller had a good business going. If it wasn't him giving me good measure, anyone of his five Barbadian girls would. Talking to him before the start of play, he said, "It will be great if Lara can break Sir Gary's record."

So, quick as a flash, I said, "Will it be drinks all round if he does succeed?"

Pretending at first to misunderstand me, he presumably had weighed up in his mind how big a loss he would take over such a deal, then, "Of course," the reply came. You could tell right from the start of play that Lara was going to try to beat the record, as both Arthurton and himself just kept the scoreboard ticking along at a nice pace to make sure nobody lost interest. That always left targets to be chatted over at drinks intervals. At lunch, I went round to see George and Isobelle.

This time I had brought my camera with me, as yesterday there was a very inquisitive Iguana who might even get near to my shutter. I placed a piece of cheese on top of the parapet wall and, very quickly, as if it knew I was a provider, he came and tried to devour it all in one go. Guessing that I would not get another chance like this, I clicked and snapped him while he almost choked on his meal.

Afternoon—just the same steady progress, Arthurton had gone for 47, Chanderpaul 41 not out, Brian Lara 320 not out, had made this West Indies score of 502 for 4 wickets look pretty formidable and safe.

Spotting the rum-seller I asked him, "Will you be here tomorrow?"

The reply: "Of course I will."

While taking my banner down, there was much excitement, as someone has nicked six bottles of his best rum and right from under the stall where he keeps the medicine. The police were buzzing around and interviewing anyone in reach of their arm. I made my way very discreetly away. Again, everybody on the coach back agrees they have seen a master craftsman at work with the bat and, again, they all look as if, like the English fielders, they have been chasing the ball around all day.

Nobody in our chalet does much during the evening after a meal, so between ten-thirty and eleven p.m. lights out.

Day 27 - Day Three of 5th and Final Test

The rain had started approximately six a.m. and as the roof of the building is made up of cedar Shingles, which is less than a quarter of an inch thick, you can gather it was quite a racket for a spell. Martin has had a rotten night again. Still the nurse is coming to see him before we go to cricket.

I made myself a couple of slices of toast and a cup of coffee. Barry has been out and come back soaking wet, saying, "I'll dry myself and then I intend to have a dip in the sea before we go–I'll go and change." I stood there scratching my head wondering, why change?

I told the others that I wanted to change some money, so I telephoned for the buggy; in less than five minutes I was up at reception, I desperately wanted to change some travellers' cheques and about six others had the same thing in mind, including Phil one of the trio from London, who told me he was an O's supporter (Leyton Orient).

"No money—we have run out, sir," came the reply on making inquiries.

There was lots of dashing about and numerous phone calls, especially as more of the group had arrived wanting money changed.

After half an hour one of the staff decides to look in the safe, which the chief cashier has looked in and said was empty. Now it has plenty of dollars. I joined a few of the others. One remarks, changing the atmosphere, "What's up? It's got two doors one at the front and one in the back. Can't be!" Everybody's happy now as very quickly we are all solvent again with right currency.

Back at 429 Martin has had a visit from the nurse who tells him he is making good progress, is going to change his medicine, but to continue with the pills, so we keep our fingers crossed.

We followed a different route to St John's, this time over bigger and better potholes. Fortunately the rain had now completely gone, only a few clouds scurrying across the sky. Yes, it looked good for Lara and cricket.

It was about twenty minutes to go before the lunch break that Lara hit his forty-fourth four to record 369. Nearly everyone with a camera was waiting at the ready for this magical moment, all with the same urge.

I clicked my action shot of the century and at exactly the same time Richard, the chap from Kent, stood up to take his. Later, when developed, a large bald patch of cranium takes up half the photo.

Lots I could say about Brian Lara's innings, but as it has been recorded so many times I'll just say, "I was there." He scored another 6 runs and was out caught by Jack Russell and bowled by Andy Caddick for 375 runs.

By the time all the excitement had died down, and the square had been tidied up, and all the travelling Trinidadians had been ushered back to their seats, after seeing their hero beat the world record, lunch was upon us.

Strolling round to George and Isobelle's, I was in for a pleasant surprise for their granddaughter Clara had arrived and was waiting to greet me. Talk about a chip off the block, she was now well on the way to be a schoolteacher too, and had almost completed her studies. I was only sorry that I could not converse with her and told her so, explaining that I had had only a local education. "Why was that?" she inquired.

"My fault entirely and nobody else's," I said. A very pleasant lunch hour I must admit.

Back at cricket, the West Indies declared at 593 for 5 wickets with Chanderpaul 75 not out. Batting straightaway after lunch, the first English wicket went at 40. Alec Stewart has been caught at deep mid-wicket, and when he went I thought, here we go again, especially as he had played so well in Barbados. I for one had such a lot of confidence in him; however, after Ramprakash had gone for 19 and the score was at 70, Atherton 63 not out and Robin Smith 68 not out, carried on until close of play both batting well and both having a good understanding with each other, the score 185 for 2 wickets.

Earlier, just after the tea interval, I went across to the rum-seller nearby who immediately recognised me, saying, "Yes, here is your rum and coke, but only you and nobody else."

I did mention to him that he promised drinks all round. It made no difference–I was the only one who had a measure, but he was pretty generous with me as I did eventually get three measures from him, I am sure. With the blood running round me from frequent walks up and down the steps, and all the bottles, cans, rum and mixes running with it, my approach to these obstacles both up and down was transformed.

Time to pick up my banner–I was untying it from the wire, when I received a tap on my shoulder and a voice said, "I want to help you, Englishman." Turning round, of course it was the rum-seller's daughter with an outfit so close to me it was doing my eyesight the world of good. As fast as I was undoing the ribbons that held the banner to the wire, she was tying it up again. I think the banner was tied up again at least six times, and both of us were in fits of laughter, I gripped one of her hands and told her, "I must go as I have to catch the coach back to the hotel, but I will see you tomorrow."

"No, you are all having a rest day tomorrow, but will you be here Wednesday?"

My reply: "Yes."

On the way back to the St James Club it poured with rain. Rentford was our driver and someone asked him, "Have you ever seen the gutters on either side full with water?"

He answered, "Nearly every time in the rainy season, when typhoons are regular visitors to our island, those gutters are overflowing–in fact the whole road is awash."

This is just what I suspected and I was mighty glad when we arrived back home. I have never been one for calculating, but if I said that at one stage of our journey the water was running level for two cricket pitches and was, as mentioned earlier, four feet wide by four feet and deep, so there was a lot of water on either side of this twelve-foot-wide carriageway—quite hair-raising to say the least.

Phil, Alan and Ken has asked Martin and me if we would like to go down to English Harbour for a meal, and share the taxi fare, share the meal expenses and share the taxi fare back. Super idea! Martin has improved a lot today and is also firmly established as Mrs Spicer's score-card maker-upper. Deposing what looked like very likely candidates all around where we were sitting, I for one would say, looking at his own immaculate one, he was an excellent choice.

It turned out to be a very reasonable evening meal and with transport it cost us 125 EC dollars each plus tip.

I had a night-cap in the bar in the main section where there is also a casino, Phil playing in there for a while and coming out with winnings, so everybody going their different ways quite late, each contented with the day's occurrences.

Day 28

6.30 a.m. Drawing the curtains, it looked a beautiful morning so I decided to have a quick dip and dry out walking along the beach. I trotted down the steps and there on the lower one was a monster crab, the one-arm species, so I quickly backpeddled to my room and got my camera. When I got back a lady from three chalets down was standing there looking at it. It was seemingly lifeless and she said to me, "Is it dead?"

I said, "No, I don't think so, but isn't it a size?"

Her next words did surprise me: "Do you think I could take a photo of you holding it up?"

This soon achieved, I carried on walking towards the sea, placing it on the sand about two feet from the water where it very quickly proved it was alive by breaking speed limits to reach it.

Back in the chalet, Barry was the first one I saw and I told him about the crab and how the lady further along had a fair knowledge of crabs, telling me that some of the bigger ones have one leg sometimes three feet in length and generally keep to their own part of the beach. You could see this had worried Barry and he must have been weighing up the possibilities of what might happen to him if he encountered one of this dimension while he was swimming.

We were all at breakfast when Barry said, "You won't see me swimming in that part of the sea anymore," as he walked out with his towel.

We are all doing our own thing today, well this morning anyway, for a Mike Burton's Cricket Extravaganza was taking place on the beach this afternoon. Quite a number of the lads have put their names down. I promised to go along and support the do.

I rang 19 for the buggy about nine, which took me to the entrance gates where making inquiries at the guard house (or similar) I heard, "No, there are no buses that go to English Harbour. If you don't want a taxi, you might get a lift."

I decided on this option so started walking and had only gone a short distance when a truck pulled up beside me and I asked the driver if he was going to English Harbour. "No," his reply, "but going within a couple of miles."

"Super."

"Jump in." He told me straightaway he was a farmer and as he was going to St Johns, he would take me there and bring me back later as he had made arrangements to pick up some goats.

I toyed with this idea for a while especially when he said, "You know, man, that no buses go to English Harbour only taxi-buses–didn't you know that?"

"No, I was not aware of that. I don't suppose it pays the bus company to run them," for although we had come some distance we had not seen any people. Arriving at a road junction with a signpost that stated English Harbour two miles, I got out and offered the farmer some money. This he refused. "Many thanks," I said and he was gone.

I was going to be lucky if I reached my destination inside two to three hours, knowing how I dawdle and ask questions, but, as I say, I only socialise.

Turning round after some ten minutes steady walking, a van came along. I waved to see if he would stop–sure thing, right beside me.

"You wanna lift, boss–jump in."

This lift could not have been improved upon for it was delivering to the only supermarket here in English Harbour. The time when I alighted was nine-thirty so I was well pleased with my thumbing. I had listened to various people's conversations about this place, yet it had never struck me how strategically important this natural harbour was to Lord Nelson (late eighteenth century). It should have rung several bells in my grey cells when briefly reading notes about the Island of Antigua, and this one in particular–Nelson's Dockyard. "WHEW!"

I paid my four dollars' entrance fee and now I was inside the dockyard I could almost have turned the clock back a couple of centuries for the place was alive with sails. But in this century, instead of man o' wars, they belonged to ocean yachts of all shapes and sizes with masts maybe forty, fifty and sixty feet or more high, each one alight with a red lamp.

Of course these were the red lights that we had all seen last night in the pitch darkness, mistaking them for lights from buildings across the harbour, or from the hills beyond. One chap had said, "Shirley Heights are in another direction, but a lot of properties though are over there." What idiots we were (and only a few glasses!).

And now as I looked up at the lamps all swaying from side to side through the continual tempo of the sea, not one but every one had joined up with its neighbour from mid-mast upwards, in an incessant gibberish chatter of yacht fastening and fittings. A make-believe world they certainly were (were they taking the mickey for quoting them unfairly?). I found a seat and started reading the brochure I had purchased on my way in.

It was here in 1674 that an Admiral of the Fleet, Sir Christopher Codrington (that rings a bell), arrived here and spotted its potential for a good base for the fleet. After his soil samples were proved successful, the whole area close by was assigned and excellent sugar cane plantations were established all over the island, giving the local labour force work that was never to end.

I was quite interested in the mention of the Dockyard Bakery, which is open to visitors for tea, et cetera, so I walked round to find it, as well as the 300-year-old sandbox tree directly in front. I purchased a pastry and a coffee, looked at the tree and, like I often do, wondered at the tales it could tell, if it could only talk.

You could quite understand why it was chosen as a dockyard, not only for the repair of ships, but also for its ability to conceal. I carried on walking and this time paid a visit to a dwelling house, not the property that Nelson is supposed to have used while on the island, but it was in quite good condition. It seemed that, when Nelson arrived here in 1777, Antigua was a busy repair dockyard for all ships with sail-size immaterial. The bigger ships passed through the entrance without difficulty, as the chain across the entrance lay on the sea bed and did not hinder the progress or interfere with the ship's draught.

The chain was only raised when danger from foreign ships threatened the station.

What a chain and what an entrance!

Horatio was just nineteen, when he arrived here. The frigate *Lowestoft* crossed the Atlantic Ocean conveying eighteen merchantmen, each carrying vital supplies, such as material for building, tools and implements for everyday use. Very quickly Horatio was made up to a Second Lieutenant, a position he was promised when he recovered from a bout of malaria. July of that year, he went to Jamaica. The Commander in charge here was Captain William Lockier, whose purpose was to get involved in active service, for it was here that the American War of Independence had broken out two years earlier. Any ships with cannon were required to make sure all the Islands that belonged to the Crown were kept free from any foreign ships that might invade. It was not necessarily engagements on the high seas with ships under another flag, but more often the private ships–pirates of course after the spoils of war.

These then–if they were captured by our frigates–those captured vessels would be enormous prizes as their treasures would be divided up, so everybody, from the captain down to the lad who ran up and down to the Crow's Nest, had a share.

In the early part of 1778, Nelson was promoted yet again to rank of Master and Commander and given the total command of a ship called *Badger*. This was a brig. And under Lord Nelson it proved just the tonic he needed and proved that he could hold his own with the best. Just like its animal namesake, she was smart, quick, a relentless pursuer and under full sail there was no equal for her size.

In the early part of 1779, he seized a French ship, full of cargo. Briefly, it seemed each ship would have all its treasures valued and each sailor would receive a share of the riches. This apparently was the case with the French capture.

After these skirmishes, you can imagine the dockyard here was very busy. The Man o' wars, frigates, brigs, et cetera would come in and have repairs or in some cases complete overhauls. Oh to have lived here when the place was a buzz.

June 1779: Nelson had promotion again. This time he was made up to post captain and given command of the frigate *Hinchenbrook*–twenty-eight guns and in charge of 200 men and just twenty years of age. Whilst he was in Jamaica a surgeon named Dr Mosely checked him over and noticed that he was going down again with his earlier illness and told him in no uncertain terms that if he did not return home to England he would not live to see many more sunsets.

The booklet concluded this early part of his life here.

This has been a marvellous inception for Horatio and it turns out to have been a wonderful experience with excellent benefits, ultimately for his battles with ships of foreign countries.

It had not taken me long to realise that I was probably sitting here, perhaps in the same place as Lord Nelson, admiring the same scene. Only the boats I was observing were for pleasure and not for fighting battles with—looking up at the flags from so many different countries I could only see friendly foes in sight.

Finding out the time was eleven-fifteen, and walking round to another part of the dockyard I found part of the original chain. I am sure I would have struggled to lift only a couple of the links. As I was making these notes—"I must find out how it was raised from the sea bed and lowered again sometime"—I thought I would go back and have another pastry and coffee. After all, if an identical one was sold here in the same ovens in 1743, there was no doubt in my mind that Horatio would have climbed these steps and maybe had one too. He had been here! And that was important to me. I have been all over his ship the *Victory* in Portsmouth so can truly say that I have again followed in his footsteps. (I wonder how much the pastry differed from those early specials!)

Restoration work here in Nelson's Dockyard started in the 1950s and has been going on ever since. It appears that climatic conditions are very favourable for preserving old buildings and even clothing.

Again, admiring this red-brick building with its superb period arches, time certainly moved back a pace. I had not noticed that part of it is also a museum and anything associated with the eighteenth century you could find here—maybe a bit dusty, but there were authentic uniforms, buttons, rusty swords, cannon balls, clay pipes, muskets plus umpteen other items. Talking to the warden in charge, I discovered in pride of place was a model ship of the line. It was a brig, and seeing also a scale sailor on board you just wonder at the improvements that the next two centuries brought to oceans the world over, and its vessels for plying the world's trade.

There was also a mid-nineteenth century schooner. It seemed very little had changed during 100 years, but what changes have been made during this last one.

Outside the building and nearby was the dry dock, massive by any standards. It impressed me for it instantly struck me that this was the exact chamber that Lord Nelson's frigate or brig had put in for repairs.

I asked a couple of local chaps where the entrance to the harbour was. Both pointed in the same direction, but as I had just come out of another building through a different door from the one I had entered by, I was not sure of my bearings so I gave up.

As buildings and places of interest go, I must say that here yesteryear was very much alive and locals did not intend to let their history desert them. What I did notice and enjoy was that where an important building had been a nice informative commemorative plaque was placed to remind you of historical events.

Checking on the time, I thought if I could get back to the supermarket, I could load up with supplies to last me over the next two days. I made my purchases and was sitting outside having a nice cool drink when an elderly couple sat down, so, as is normal, we all started talking. He told me that they were both from the Midlands originally and had supported Notts for a lifetime. They had lived here in Antigua for ten years and now were very much retired.

I told him I was from Essex and before I had time to tell him that I only support the county occasionally, he had gone through the whole of the Essex XI, plus others, finally asking me if I knew who was the overseas player that they are signing from Australia this coming season. For the life of me I could not remember who it was and told him so saying, "I am afraid that you are like some of the chaps in our tour party, know more about my county than I do."

He still continued asking me questions about Brian Taylor, et cetera. I could see that the conversation was getting out of my depth, so I politely told him that I had to go and wished them well and scarpered. (I later found out the player in question: KASPROWICZ.)

Seeing some people I knew who were from the St James Club Complex, I discovered they too were going back so I asked them if I could share the taxi-bus with them and share the cost. "Yes, of course." Arriving back and a buggy ride down to 429, the time was now two p.m. Within five minutes I was in the sea, where I stopped for three-quarters of an hour.

Before I entered the water I had drawn some lines along the sand, just to see if they would disappear whilst I was in the sea, since each time I went in and out of the water the shoreline never seemed to alter. On looking at them when I came out, I am sure there was no difference, the water's edge remained in the same position as when I first went in. So this proved one thing—there was hardly any tide, if any.

First thing in the morning, I would have another look to make sure.

By the time I had changed and walked about 100 yards along the beach where the cricket match was now in progress. It was just a match between ourselves (no I did not take part) and everybody had a bat and ball. Tom Graveney was the umpire. When everyone had had an innings and a bowl, he was asked if he would like a knock. "Yes, why not," was his reply. You could see that Jackie his wife, sitting on a deckchair, did not approve of Tom's gesture. It was only a soft ball and I for one had noticed some pretty quick bowlers amongst the group of lads, probably an ambition with all of them to knock the great man's stump down.

Now I am not exaggerating over what I witnessed that lovely afternoon on the beach at St James Club, and anyone who reads this in the future would agree that Tom had not lost his touch–of that there was no doubt. All the fielders were scattered around and along the beach with three permanently in the sea, waiting to swim out and retrieve the ball so there was very little hold-up. Tom had smashed his third delivery to mid-wicket and as this was on his near side and in the sea this was the spot he placed it at unusually regular intervals. I don't know how many people had noticed, but each time Tom was whacking the ball just that little bit harder, and, of course, this gave everybody including Tom a breather. This was fine until he smashed one, timing to perfection, twice the distance of his first whacks. One swimmer said to his two companions, "I am not fetching that," the other two agreeing one saying to Tom, "Go and get it yourself."

You had to agree with Tom when he said, "Think it's time to pack up."

Several duckings now started taking place the first one

being Julie the girl in charge, I daresay some fifty of us thoroughly enjoyed the afternoon.

Martin, I must say, is much better, but our other flatmate, Phil? Is he brewing for something as he is trying his hardest to keep whatever lurgie it might be at bay by making some ear-bursting sounds on the conch he has purchased. He has me in fits of laughter with this at times.

Nobody is moving far; each of us cooks something different, banks and cokes seem to be the popular liquid refreshments, toasted cheese and meat sandwiches are the mainstay meal. Early bed ten-thirty.

Day 29 - 4th day of 5th Test

I had a walk along the beach and looked for the marks I had made; only one had gone so the rise and fall over sixteen hours was less than twelve inches.

Back in 429, we all had a buggy ride up to the main complex for breakfast this morning. Mind you it was twice the price at twenty-one EC dollars, but you could help yourself to as much as you wanted so my trusty carrier came in handy for the oranges, plums, grapes, et cetera. The coach left at eight-thirty-three, arriving near the ground just after nine. I wanted to locate a bank for I was running short of money. This did not take long and I was soon back at the turnstiles, I went in, sat in my seat and straightaway over the loudspeaker an announcement was made: "Will all those supporters who are sitting in the new Andy Roberts Stand please leave immediately." No one at first knew or guessed what had happened until a whisper went round that a bomb had been planted under a seat in our stand.

It was quite orderly; outside two chaps who had not

entered the ground asked me, "What's up? Have England declared?"

I said, "That would have been even a bigger shock than the present one."

"What happened then for all the people to leave the ground?" the taller chap asked.

"A bomb scare," I said.

"What! It can't be—we have come from a long way away to take photos of the cricket. How the hell are we going to take some shots from out here? Who put the bomb there? Is it a big bomb, where is it?"

I moved away scratching my head.

It did not take long for the stand to be declared safe for the supporters to return to their seats, and it did not delay the start of play as it got underway on time.

Atherton and Smith stayed together for all the morning's play, both batting well and not at all worried by the West Indian quick bowlers.

Lunch-time, I went round to George and Isobelle's to have my bagels and beers. As I walked through the gate, I could hear the cricket on the wireless and a commentator talking about the bomb scare and its implications. This was the time when I found out that all was not harmony around the island for George didn't half lay into the government and its failings, telling me that they waste money on improvements that are not beneficial to any of them, and without their sanction. It was a grave misuse of money: "In fact I don't know how the road users stand for it, for the roads are definitely deteriorating by the day."

There then followed a long complaint about the potholes that I was witness to, George saying that round St

John's they are quite respectable, but then as you go further out so they get deeper and wider, each time you drive over them. He said, "I do know something—I will not vote for them again." I could see by the large clock that I must go and so say, "Many thanks, see you tomorrow." Both of them say, "It's a jolly good match."

Back at cricket, it was about three-fifteen that Atherton was out for 135. This stand between him and Smith of 303 had broken an England third wicket record, Smith going on to score 175 and by the close of play England were 442 for 6 wickets, so it looked very unlikely if there was going to be a definite result now.

Taking my banner down, Vincia the Antiguian girl was busy getting involved with me again and this time came straight out with, "I want you to take me to England."

The banner came down pretty quick, with me saying, "See you tomorrow—I have to catch our coach."

Back on the coach, several are making arrangements for a visit to English Harbour for a meal and a few beers; time to meet will be seven-forty-five, all to share a taxi-bus or two.

Later, down at the Admiral's Inn, the recommended eating place approved by others of our group, it was soon even later still! I don't know how management stood for all the noise that continued unabated for a couple of hours. Mind you, they took some dollars off us, so I daresay they accepted with some tolerance this noisy lot of English cricket supporters.

I must mention of course the interior furbishments of the Admiral's Inn. As you looked around, very present were the vibes of the eighteenth and nineteenth centuries—ceiling timbers, doors and walls, everywhere you cast an eye. The table where fifteen of us were sitting looked as if it had come straight off a ship of the line. I know at the time I wondered if dancing wenches had ever done a turn on this massive piece of history, and I was only sorry that those waitresses attending us were not wearing the appropriate clothing for the period. One in particular, I am positive, would not have needed much encouragement to give us all a whirl, and as the evening progressed this began to look highly probable (no such luck). It would have been nice too for our beers to be served up in pewter pots, again no joy.

Last orders were shouted, so it was now time for the accountants in the company to get their heads together. Everyone had a different price tag and the ninety-five dollars concluded was quite reasonable. I might also add that in this costing there had been several bottled export beers. We have discovered when we visit these hotel diners that they certainly vary in price. Here they were four times the price of local beers and that was reasonable.

Back at the main complex at twelve-twenty.

Day 30 - 5th and final day of Fifth Test

Up at six-thirty, quick dip in the sea, then a good long walk, which took me further round the Bay and well past where the rubbish was disposed of. For several days I had wanted to look at a partially completed building, a little way up from the beach. I considered enquiring and seeing a chap nearby looking after the cattle I asked him, "Has the firm run out of money. What's the reason for the hold-up?"

"No, what has happened, man, is because all the workers have gone to St John's to see the cricket—the boss is an ex-West Indian cricketer. Now all he does is buy land and build apartment blocks here on the island."

Looking around at the cattle grazing, I said, "Surely not here, isn't there any Green Belt?"

"What's that, man?"

Back at 429 I make myself some buttered toast. Very few of the other inhabitants are about, nobody in the sea and it's looking extremely unlikely that anyone will make the journey across the island. However, later on we all take the buggy up, with Martin much improved but still a bit jaded. Arriving at the pick-up point, we find that only a handful of the group are going to see the last day's play.

The coach left at eight-fifteen, and Mrs Spicer was one of us and her poor face is getting redder each time I see her. I said to her, "I'm surprised to see you as I thought you might be doing some last-minute shopping."

"Percy, you don't think I am going to miss the last day's play, do you?"

It was indeed a dismal day's cricket and during the lunch break I went round to see George and Isobelle for the last time. His eldest son was there and on seeing him I nearly put my foot in it, for I considered straightaway that he was a clergyman, seeing that he was dressed all in black and wearing a type of dog collar. George guessing my assumption said, "This is Charles and he is in the funeral business."

I carried on eating my bagels and drinking my beers and as Charles appeared to have very little interest in cricket, and me similarly showing no inclination to converse about undertaking, the conversation had almost slowed right up. Finally, completing my lunch break, I politely said, "I must go as I don't want to miss any of the action," and shaking all their hands, we all wished each other well, they trusting that I would have a safe journey home.

At the conclusion of play as the knowledgeable ones had predicted–that a draw was the only outcome of the game–England had scored the same as the West Indies, 593, so the West Indies went in again and scored 43 without loss.

The man of the match was Brian Lara and Curtly Ambrose was man of the whole series. From the start of play, Banks, rum and mixes were the order of the day, so I concluded this test match in hearty mood and can record that everyone is pleased with the result. Both sides' supporters were in jovial mood and I'm sure everyone in the stands were now out on the pitch, each one offering the other's hand in friendship, be they erstwhile friends or foes.

While I was out on the field I was talking to a local chap who reminded me about the convicts in the prison nearby, telling me that all sorts of villains are kept locked up there. For some strange reason I said to him, "Are there any witch doctors in there?" I daresay at the back of my mind was the last statement that Rudolf the coconut man had made to me when we were about to leave Barbados!

"Witch doctors, nearly every other person in the wing that looks towards the cricket field is one of them. They're always casting spells on every other person especially those that are sports-inclined, for they cannot abide anyone doing exorcisms, man. Why do you ask?"

I so much wanted to stop and find out a bit more of this chicanery, for I had witnessed some of this for real in the last few days. When we saw a chap called Gravey performing in the main stand to voluptuous applause from every corner of the ground and no doubt very warmly from those inmates who could see through their barred windows, I had a good excuse to get away for as yet I still had not retrieved my banner from the fence.

I was very pleased on the way there when I took a photo of my room-mate while he was busy taking a photo of the great man himself, Brian Lara, receiving his award, surrounded by umpteen well-wishers.

I had started to untie my banner when several voices called out, "The Englishman is here." Within a second or two of that call, Vincia was beside me helping to undo, or rather retie the banner I was trying to take down and fold up. I must say she had pulled out all the stops to impress me that it was going to be very worthwhile following her suggestion from yesterday to take her back home with me. I was keeping an eye open, for I assumed she must have brothers and sisters, uncles and aunts, when she slipped a piece of paper in my hand saying, "There's my address, Percy, please write."

Confusion reigned.

I then said, "I'll tell you what I will do, I'll take your photo. Then, now I have your address, I will send it on to you. How's that?"

"Oh, thank you."

A sort of calm had now been restored. The banner had been retrieved and put in my carrier, then I was saying goodbyes to all the family now gathered. I was walking to the coach when I saw a very important person coming towards me with two big chaps in attendance. I took my camera out of its case, stopped him dead in his tracks and said, "Excuse me, Prime Minister, could I have your photograph?"

An instant look of dissent appeared on both the bouncers' faces. A big smile beamed out from the VIP's face: "Why of course."

A click of the shutter, and with a "Many thanks", I continued on my way knowing I had captured on film the top man himself, the Hon Lester Bird, also Minister of Foreign Affairs and Social Affairs.

I walked to the coach to find there were even fewer people on board than had come up this morning. Martin is much improved. Tonight was going to be a bit special for Mike Burton was putting on a Gala Dinner in the St James Club, collar and tie, nobody to be late—seven-thirty sharp. Back in 429 at five, I knew what I had to do to cool off a very excited pack of grey cells—no more turmoil, but to cure my slight disorientation, I knew the right place for cooling down!

I went straight into the sea and stopped there for a good half an hour making sure that I was giving myself a nice going-away present, it also working wonders for a very disturbed brain.

We were nearly ready to ring for the buggy when we heard a knock on the door. Edith the maid came in with more sugar cane for me. I thought I'd already had my quota, not so.

"Is this enough?

"Yes, that's plenty," came my reply.

Then she brought out from her shopping bag two bottles of rum, in fact exactly the same kind as two I had purchased earlier—real good quality ones from a supermarket in St John's.

I found thirty dollars, which for some reason she only

accepted with reluctance.

I said to the others, "I'll take one of those up to the do," placing it in my carrier.

"You will never get away with that, not up there in the dining suite," all three said.

When our transport arrived, I must say what a transformation the chalet's inmates had undergone–all spruced up, collars and ties, each intending not to let the side down for Mike Burton's farewell dinner.

Putting my bottle in the faithful carrier, the buggy was called and on arrival at the main entrance Phil says, "What have you got in your carrier, Perc, seashells?"

I let him have a look inside.

"A bottle of rum. I have something to go with that," he said, "I'll go and get it." As his room was nearby, he was soon back with a large plastic bottle of coke.

All agreed: "Super."

Everything at the dinner was freebies, the wine as well, red or white. I am no wine expert, but would consider what we had was rubbish and am sure if the boss man himself had been there no way would he have paid for that. While I am on a grumble, which I am pleased to say is very infrequent, the main course consisted of very measly portions. In fact if they had put another serving on my plate you would still have room for much more.

During the evening banquet, interlaced with pleasantries from Tom Graveney who was our Master of Ceremonies, he also gave us an excellent farewell speech. To this the applause he received was loud and long. I was surprised when my name was called out in what had been called the Honours list. The award was for wearing the same shirt for every one of the fifteen days of test cricket, noticed because it had been seen regularly with the Mike Burton Logo.

I don't mind telling you I was taken aback by this. When I was asked to make a speech about this, I replied very emphatically, "I am sure others were doing the same and can assure all of you that that shirt had come off my back at nightfall, been washed, dried through the night and then drip dried, and so was ready for the following day's enterprises."

The waiters who were buzzing around seemed to be quite friendly and when I asked one if he could let us have a few glasses for our rum and cokes, he quickly obliged, returning with nearly a dozen. When the bottle was offered round to nearby tables and its strength reported, most abstained, so it was left to our table and one or two others who arrived with a glass wanting to sample our wares.

All of this part of the evening was quite clear to me. I remember receiving an invitation from another Dave, Assistant Master of Ceremonies, and walking up, standing on a chair and quoting several verses of Pam Ayres "I wish I'd looked after my teeth". I know I was applauded for this and there was, to my recollection, no other noises. Sid the chap from South London quoted, "I wish I'd been a barrow boy years ago" and our other room-mate Barry sang, "I did it my way", again to much applause. I do know something: that my attention-drawing behaviour is something I could never indulge in back home. I think it is very strange, and others agree that I only indulge in such pleasurable conduct in places where I am not known, and I know I'm far from home.

Twelve-thirty: we have all been told to clear out of the

dining room as the staff wanted to clear up and make the place presentable for tomorrow. I go with several others to the bar where I sit on a high stool and each time I am asked to join them in a drink, I am not one to refuse, so I oblige–another rum and mix. "WHEW!"

Two-fifteen: time please! I remember walking along the passage to pick up the buggy waiting below the steps.

The next thing I recall?–For a start, total darkness. I slurred, "What's going on?" as I found both my hands were tightly gripped by two separate ones. Phil from Bristol was holding one and Martin the other. It was Martin who said, "You have fallen down the main steps and you're now on the way to hospital at St Johns."

I then remember a wheelchair and being sat in it and wheeled wherever, a chap in a pair of shorts, then not a lot more until the journey back to the St James Club when I heard Martin say, "We have just gone over a pothole."

I was told later that it was four-forty-five when they put me to bed.

I must have gone straight off to sleep, for when I opened my eyes the sun was streaming in through the window facing me. I was told by a lot of anxious faces round the bed that the time was eight-thirty–and I could not "Christmas Eve it". Barry stood there with a cup of tea in his hand for me.

I am sure that this was the best cuppa that I have ever tasted.

Now gradually recovering some of senses, Martin tells me that I have six stitches in my eyebrow where it had split open when I fell down eight steps in the front of the main entrance. It was him and Phil who had held me on the ride across to St Johns. "As there were no ambulances available we had to travel in a Dormobile. This was the reason why we had to hang on to you so tightly as you might have fallen out!" I thank them both. Martin then says, "Have you looked in the mirror yet?"

"No, but I suppose I had better." Getting out of bed and going to the bathroom, I have a quick look at my visage. What a mess!—especially the large sticky plaster that was now showing signs of wear and tear.

Back in the main room Phil says, "We are going home today so we'd better start packing." This had more effect on me than any medicine anyone could have given me.

"We are going home today!" As the bathroom was now empty, I had a quick shower (not feeling well enough to have a final dip). With this completed, I felt heaps better and told the boys I was going for a quick walk along the beach, as my head was far from being its old self. When I returned all the lads were ready for breakfast, so a buggy was called, for we had all decided to have it up at the main complex.

All the group came over and asked how I was, intent on seeing for themselves what damage had been done and how I was feeling. Several asked me about the other chap, how did he get on? Up to this stage and even beyond and on the plane, I for some reason was sure someone pushed me. Me fall down some tiled steps—never!

My mind must have been at sixes and sevens for when I had completed my breakfast of just a bowl of cornflakes, I came away without taking any fruit.

A buggy ride back, so everyone is under the weather I'm sure, be it last night's beverages or the fact that we are into our last hours on this paradise—nobody's walking. I got stuck in to my packing straightaway and made sure that the four bottles of rum (159 per cent proof) were carefully wrapped up in newspapers, likewise my sugar canes. I finally completed my packing with a few of the club's face towels. TWO!

Martin is now getting over his tummy bug, and I know from their attitudes that Phil and Barry are not looking forward to going home. Martin reminds me that I have to visit the nurse somewhere higher up in the complex if I want to replace the plaster round my eye.

So I walk up the several levels to her mini-hospital which evidently caters for everyone inside and outside the holiday resort. When I reached there the nurse asked right away what I had been up to and I told her that "someone had pushed me down some steps, the main entrance ones".

Whilst she was taking off the old dressing and replacing it with a new one she told me that she had done all her training in England at a hospital called Broomfield in Essex. "Where do you come from?"

I told her, "That's where I come from—Essex—and I know of that hospital. It's near Bishops Stortford, which is only about fifteen miles from where I live near Loughton."

I must say after she had completed my dressing, my face had much improved, yet it still looked as if it has been run over. I thanked her most kindly and she refused the dollars that I offered. Spotting a large tin which said "HELP" on the side, I put a few dollars inside.

Back at 429, the annex apartment we had all shared for the past nine days, it had now been left reasonably tidy. I don't mind saying that I had come to this part of the world without any idea of what this mini paradise was likely to be. The lads were still moving around as if mesmerised, Phil unsure about whether he should put the conch in his large suitcase, or the hand-luggage one. Barry has had his final dip and says to me, "Come on and have a last swim." I could not face it.

I did sit out on the patio for the last time and looked all around at the solitude and enchanting picture-book surroundings–the whole bay itself, the few yachts, the three landing stages. Across the knockout blue water was the hilly stretch of Shirley Heights, an area I had seen on the maps, but failed to find the time to visit to discover its treasures. My eye ranged round to the right where the unfinished building was, now buzzing with workmen, the few cattle having a munch on what I could remember was only dead or dying vegetation; then again, a quick flash right the way round–tranquillity and peacefulness abounded. On hearing a call from Martin, "Come on, it's time to go," I made my way slowly inside 429 closing the French windows for the last time, wondering if I would ever again set foot in or on Marmora Bay, Antigua.

One p.m.: the buggy arrived to take us up to headquarters, some of us to square accounts and me meeting many more who enquired after my health. Even then it was another one and a half hours until the coach arrived to take us on the twenty-minute journey to the VC Bird International Airport. It took us a long time to get through to Departures, only to have to wait some more, or walk about like I do, watching the clock most of the time. Not so today, for perfect strangers were coming up to me asking after my well-being since the night's adventure. I suppose, in truth, I had got myself a bad name and reputation when I went to the wrong airport, thus missing the flight at the start of my holiday.

I did sit down and, whilst drinking a beer by myself,

cast my mind over who had been in my group and the other groups. In my own company were postal workers, accountants, ex rail personnel, travel reps, folk from the motor trade and retired folk from all parts of the country; Bristol, London, Northampton, Warwickshire, Yorkshire, the boys from Wales, the lads from Scotland and Ireland– all compatriots who had a burning desire to see England win a test match and series on foreign soil. Failing that, they wanted to have a good time and put up with the good-humoured banter and ribbing that comrades-in-arms of the bat and ball suffer.

No doubt embarrassed, like the occasion at Port of Spain, the times I have said to myself and others of the same mind IF! (That tiny word that has given so many highs and lows through my lifetime.) IF we had bowled and fielded last, would Caddick, Lewis and Fraser have exploited the conditions like Curtly Ambrose and Courtney Walsh had done? I thought of my own limited knowledge of county and test cricket players and results, compared with what I had picked up in the company of a few of the amateur experts, listening to conversations when subjects of this nature are discussed. Conversations like this have been, not so much who an individual played for, but when, how many times an England Cap, details on test cricketers going back yonks. I recall Sid from South London telling me that he was only twelve years old when he saw Len Hutton score his 364 runs at the Oval in 1938, so you can see a cricket brain and memory had formed as early as that. Cricket forums, I am told, on tours have to be attended to be believed. Martin's prize possession is now his Score Book, which meticulously records every ball that had been bowled at Bridgetown and St Johns, amazing when you take into consideration how much he had been under the weather after he had captured that "tummy bug"–and then not satisfied with doing his own he also did Mrs Enid Spicer's as well.

I rest my case.

At five-forty-five p.m. approximately, our plane took off for home, most everyone fed up to the eyebrows with the long time we had been waiting. I so much wanted to doze off, but I just could not. My headache had long gone and was now replaced by a dull ache, yet my head was still clear enough to register my thoughts. The hotels that had been allotted to us–quality? Yes! But missing warmth. Telly Kelly, Julie and Roseanne, our travel managers, suffering at times yet always prepared well for misfortunes. Tom Graveney and Jackie his wife were excellent tour hosts. Gravey, I'm sorry I have not given more coverage of his aerobics during lunch breaks. I also vividly recall the Shooting Star. Gerald, David and myself were enjoying a glass on the patio at the Barbados Hilton and one of our company declared that was a powerful flash on a camera; Gerald a more than reasonable photographer had a very hearty chuckle! The tickets that Roseanne had lost duly turned up with new ticket-holders, them saying they had paid well over the face value to get the seats. As it turned out there were plenty of empty seats.

Other things I remember: Martin's account of the doctor who attended me at St John's, fixing me up dressed in a pair of shorts; my banner after I had taken it down following the deluge at Port of Spain (what a mess where all the artwork had mingled in colours that defies the imagination); the imprint of the cricket ball that made history as it was one of the fours that came off Curtly

Ambrose's bat during his stay at the wicket in West Indies second knock.

We arrived at Gatwick at about seven a.m. putting the clocks forward by five hours.

Saying goodbye to all the company of friends I had made whilst I was abroad, again I was reminded by a stranger from another group when he said, "I saw you run on the pitch at Bridgetown."

Phil, Alan, Ken, Martin and myself were all travelling on the Gatwick Express and while we were on it I received back the other two bottles of rum that Alan and Martin had brought through Customs for me, now restored to my suitcase.

At Victoria Station we say cheerio to each other, accompanied by warm hand-shakes, concluding with, "We shall have to do that again sometime, see you in Australia next winter..."

The Wisden Trophy, 1993/94, 1st Test

West Indies v England
Sabina Park, Kingston, Jamaica
19, 20, 21, 23, 24 February 1994 (5-day match)

Result: West Indies won by 8 Wickets
              West Indies leads the 5-Test series 1-0

Toss: England
Umpires: S A Bucknor and I D Robinson (Zim)
Match Referee: S M Gavaskar (Ind)
Man of the Match: J C Adams

Close of Play:
Day 1:   England 209/7 (Maynard 24, Caddick 3)
Day 2:   England 234, West Indies 238/4 (Athurton 113,
             Adams 21)
Day 3:   West Indies 407, England 80/4 (Hick 24,
             Russell 6)
Day 4:   England 267, West Indies 87/2 (Haynes 40)

The Wisden Trophy

England and lst innings

B

MA Atherton	c Murray	b KCG Benjamin	55	189
AJ Stewart	c Murray	b KCG Benjamin	70	118
GP Thorpe		b KCG Benjamin	16	69
RA Smith		b Walsh	0	6
GA Hick		b Adams	23	65
MP Maynard	lbw	b KCG Benjamin	35	68
·RC Russell	lbw	b KCG Benjamin	0	4
CC Lewis	c Adams	b Ambrose	8	27
AR Caddick	c Adams	b KCG Benjamin	3	27
AP Igglesden	not out		3	
DE Malcolm	run out		6	5
Extras	(b 2, lb 5, w 4, nb 4)		15	
Total	(all out, 98.1 overs)		234	

FOW:　1-121 (Stewart), 2-133 (Atherton), 3-134 (Smith), 4-172 (Hick), 5-172 (Thorpe), 6-172 (Russell), 7-194 (Lewis), 8-209 (Caddick), 9-227 (Maynard), 10-234 (Malcolm).

Bowling	O	M	R	W
Ambrose	22	8	46	1
Walsh	23	6	41	1
KCC Benjamin	24	7	66	6
WKM Benjamin	19.1	7	43	0
Adams	10	1	31	1

West Indies 1st Innings

DL Haynes	c Thorpe	b Malcolm	4
PV Simmons	c Russell	b Caddick	8
RB Richardson	c Maynard	b Malcolm	5
BC Lara		b Hick	83
KLT Athurton	c Lewis	b Malcolm	126
JC Adams not out			95
·JR Murray	lbw	b Igglesden	34
WKM Benjamin		b Caddick	38
CEL Ambrose		b Caddick	0
KCG Benjamin		b Lewis	0
CA Walsh	lbw	b Lewis	0
Extras	(lb 10, w 1, nb 3)		14
Total	(all out, 123 overs)		407

FoW: 1-12 (Haynes), 2-12 (Simmons), 3-23 (Richardson), 4-167 (Lara), 5-256 (Arthurton), 6-319 (Murray), 7-389 (WKM Benjamin), 8-389 (Ambrose), 9-390 (KCG Benjamin), 10-407 (Walsh)

Bowling	O	M	R	W
Malcolm	23	3	113	3
Caddick	29	5	94	3
Lewis	26	4	82	2
Igglesden	24	5	53	1
Hick	21	4	55	1

England 2nd innings

MA Atherton	c Adams	b Walsh	28
AJ Stewart	run out	KCG Benjamin)	19
RA Smith	c Adams	b Walsh	2
GA Hick	c sub	b KCG Benjamin	96
Mp Maynard	c Murray	b WKM Benjamin	0
RC Russell	c Adams	b WKM Benjamin	32
GP Thorpe		b WKM Benjamin	14
CC Lewis	lbw	b Ambrose	21
AR Caddick	not out		29
AP Igglesden	c Adams	b KCG Benjamin	0
DE Malcolm	b Walsh		18
Extras	(b 1, lb 3, w 2, nb 2)		8
Total	(all out, 91.5 overs)		267

FoW: 1-34 (Stewart), 2-39 (Smith), 3-58 (Atherton), 4-63 (Maynard), 5-126 (Russell), 6-155 (Thorpe), 7-213 (Lewis), 8-226 Hick), 9-228 (Igglesden), 10-267 (Malcolm).

Bowling	O	M	R	W
Ambrose	24	4	67	1
Walsh	24.5	6	67	3
WKM Benjamin	20	3	56	3
KCG Benjamin	18	2	60	2
Adams	2	0	9	0
Simmons	3	1	4	0

West Indies 2ⁿᵈ innings (target: 95 runs)

DL Haynes	not out		43
PV Simmons	lbw	b Igglesden	12
BC Lara		b Caddick	28
RB Richardson	not out		4
Extras	(b 5, 1b 3)		8
Total	(2 wickets, 26.2 overs)		95

DNB: KLT Arthurton, JC Adams, JR Murray, WKM Benjamin, CEL Ambrose, KCG Benjamin, CA Walsh.

FoW: 1-38 (Simmons), 2-87 (Lara)

Bowling	O	M	R	W
Malcolm	5	1	19	0
Caddick	6	1	19	1
Lewis	3	0	6	0
Igglesden	7	0	36	1
Hick	3	1	2	0
Stewart	2.2	0	5	0

The Wisden Trophy, 1993/94, 2nd Test

West Indies v England
Bourda, Georgetown, Guyana
17, 18, 19, 20, 22 March 1994 (5-day match)

Result: West Indies won by an innings and 44 runs
West Indies leads the 5-Test series 2-0

Toss: West Indies
Umpires: CR Duncan and S Venkataraghavan (Ind)
Match Referee: JR Reid (NZ)
Test Debuts: S Chanderpaul (WI)
Man of the Match: BC Lara

Close of Play:
Day 1:   England 258/5 (Atherton 131, Salisbury)
Day 2:   England 322, West Indies 152/1 (Haynes 53,
           Lara 57)
Day 3:   West Indies 487/6 (Adams 102,
           WKM Benjamin 37)
Day 4:   West Indies 556, England 119/4 (Stewart 72,
           Thorpe 10)

England 1ˢᵗ innings

MA Atherton	c Murray	b Ambrose	144
AJ Stewart		b Walsh	0
MR Ramprakash	lbw	b Walsh	2
RA Smith	c Lara	b KCG Benjamin	84
GA Hick	c Richardson	b Ambrose	33
GP Thorpe		b Ambrose	0
IDK Salisbury	lbw	b WKM Benjamin	8
RC Russell	c Richardson	b Ambrose	13
CC Lewis	c Richardson	b KCG Benjamin	17
ARC Fraser	not out		0
AP Igglesden		b KCG Benjamin	0
Extras	(lb 14, nb 7)		21
Total	(all out, 124.5 overs)		322

FoW: 1-0 (Stewart), 2-2 (Ramprakash), 3-173 (Smith), 4-245 (Hick), 5-253 (Thorpe), 6-276 (Atherton), 7-281 (Salisbury), 8-322 (Russell), 9-322 (Lewis), 10-322 (Igglesden).

Bowling	O	M	R	W
Ambrose	30	8	58	4
Walsh	26	7	69	2
KCG Benjamin	23.5	5	60	3
WKM Benjamin	26	9	62	1
Adams	3	1	10	0
Chanderpaul	16	2	49	0

The Wisden Trophy

West Indies 1st innings

DL Haynes	c Russell	b Salisbury	63
RB Richardson	c Lewis	b Fraser	35
BC Lara	c Atherton	b Lewis	167
KLT Atherton	c Thorpe	b Salisbury	5
JC Adams lbw		b Igglesden	137
S Chanderpaul		b Salisbury	62
JR Murray	lbw	b Salisbury	0
WKM Benjamin		b Fraser	44
CEL Ambrose	c Russell	b Lewis	10
KCG Benjamin	c Russell	b Lewis	1
CA Walsh		not out	10
Extras	(b 2, lb 6, w 1, nb 13)		22
Total	(all out, 153.3 overs)		556

FoW: 1-63, 2-177, 3-203, 4-315, 5-441,
6-441, 7-505, 8-520, 9-532, 10-556

Bowling	O	M	R	W
Lewis	28	1	110	3
Igglesden	24.3	3	94	1
Fraser	29	5	85	2
Salisbury	37	4	163	4
Hick	20	1	61	0
Ramprakash	15	1	35	0

England 2nd innings

MA Atherton	b Ambrose	0
AJ Stewart	b KCG Benjamin	
		79
MR Ramprakash	b Ambrose	5

RA Smith	c Richardson	b Ambrose	24
GA Hick	b KCG	Benjamin	5
GP Thorpe	b Walsh		20
·RC Russell	c Murray	b Ambrose	6
CC Lewis	c Adams	b KCG Benjamin	24
IDK Salisbury		b Walsh	19
ARC Fraser		b KCG Benjamin	0
AP Igglesden		not out	1
Extras	(b 2, lb 2, w 1, nb 2		7
Total	(all out, 85 overs)		190

FoW: 1-0 (Atherton), 2-30 (Ramprakash), 3-91 (Smith), 4-96 (Hick), 5-129 (Stewart), 6-140 (Thorpe), 7-150 (Russell), 8-185 (Lewis), 9-186 (Fraser), 10-190 (Salisbury).

Bowling	O	M	R	W
Ambrose	23	5	37	4
Walsh	25	4	71	2
				(1nb)
WKM Benjamin	16	4	44	0
KCG Benjamin	19	6	34	4
				(1nb 1w)
Adams	2	2	0	0

RA Smith: 84 runs, 160 ball, 11x4, 1x6
MA Atherton: 144 runs, 296 balls, 412 min., 17x4
CC Lewis hit 1 six
BC Lara: 167 runs, 210 balls, 25x4, 2x6
JC Adams' 100: 196 balls, 301 min., 16x4
2nd innings: Stewart hit 13 boundaries, Thorpe 3

The Wisden Trophy, 1993/94, 3rd Test

West Indies v England

Queens Park Oval, Port of Spain, Trinidad
25, 26, 27, 29, 30 March 1994 (5-day match)

Result: West Indies won by 147 runs
West Indies leads the 5-Test series 3-0

Toss: West Indies
Umpires: SA Bucknor and S Venkataraghavan (Ind_
Match Referee: JR Reid (NZ)

Close of Play:
Day 1:   West Indies 227/7 (Murray 22, Ambrose 5)
Day 2:   West Indies 252, England 236/5 (Thorpe 64,
           Russell 17)
Day 3:   England 328, West Indies 143/5
           (Chanderpaul 1)
Day 4:   West Indies 269, England 40/8 (Lewis 1)

West Indies 1ˢᵗ innings

DL Haynes		b Salisbury	38
RB Richardson	lbw	b Salisbury	63
BC Lara	lbw	b Lewis	43
KLT Arthurton	lbw	b Lewis	1
JC Adams c Smith		b Lewis	2
S Chanderpaul		b Fraser	19
JR Murray		not out	27
WKM Benjamin		b Fraser	10
CEL Ambrose	c Thorpe	b Fraser	13
KCG Benjamin		b Fraser	9
CA Walsh	lbw	b Lewis	0
Extras		(b 1, lb 13, w 1, nb 12)	27
Total		(all out, 95.2 overs)	252

FoW: 1-66 (Haynes), 2-158 (Richardson), 3-158 (Lara), 4-163 (Adams), 5-164 (Arthurton), 6-201 (Chanderpaul), 7-212 (WKM Benjamin), 8-241 (Ambrose), 9-251 (KCG Benjamin), 10-252 (Walsh).

Bowling	O	M	R	W
Fraser	24	9	49	4
Caddick	19	5	43	0
Lewis	25.2	3	61	4
Salisbury	22	4	72	2
Ramprakash	2	1	8	0
Hick	3	1	5	0

England 1ˢᵗ innings

MA Atherton	c Murray	b WKM Benjamin	48
AJ Stewart		b Ambrose	6
MR Ramprakash		c & b WK Benjamin	23
RA Smith	lbw	b Ambrose	12
GA Hick	lbw	b Walsh	40
GP Thorpe	c Lara	b Ambrose	86
RC Russell		b Ambrose	23
CC Lewis		b Ambrose	9
IDK Salisbury	c Lara	b Walsh	36
AR Caddick	c Lara	b WKM Benjamin	6
ARC Fraser	not out		8
Extras	(b 10, lb 9, w 1, nb 11)		31
Total:	(All out, 112.2 overs)		328

FoW: 1-16, 2-82, 3-87, 4-115, 5-167,
       6-249, 7-273, 8-281, 9-294, 10-328.

Bowling	O	M	R	W
Ambrose	29	6	60	5
Walsh	27.2	3	77	2
KCG Benjamin	20	5	70	0
WKM Benjamin	24	0	18	0
Adams	4	0	18	0
Chanderpaul	5	0	13	0
Arthurton	3	0	5	0

West Indies 2nd innings

DL Haynes		b Lewis	19
RB Richardson		c & b Caddick	3
BC Lara	c Salisbury	b Caddick	12
KLT Arthurton	c Stewart	b Caddick	42
JC Adams c Russell	b Salisbury		43
S Chanderpaul	c Fraser	b Caddick	50
JR Murray	c Russell	b Caddick	14
WKM Benjamin	c Fraser	b Lewis	35
CEL Ambrose	b Caddick		12
KCG Benjamin	not out		5
CA Walsh	lbw	b Lewis	1
Extras	(b 8, lb 13, nb 12)		33
Total	(all out, 87.5 overs)		269

FoW: 1-15, 2-37, 3-51, 4-131, 5-143,
6-167, 7-227, 8-247, 9-267, 10-269.

Bowling	O	M	R	W
Fraser	25	6	71	0
Caddick	26	5	65	6
Lewis	27.5	6	71	3
Salisbury	9	1	41	1

The Wisden Trophy

England 2nd innings (target: 194 runs)

MA Atherton	lbw	b Ambrose	0
AJ Stewart		b Ambrose	18
MR Ramprakash		run out	1
RA Smith		b Ambrose	0
GA Hick	c Murray	b Ambrose	6
GP Thorpe		b Ambrose	3
IDK Salisbury	c Lara	b Walsh	0
RC Russell	c sub (PV Simmons)	b Ambrose	4
CC Lewis	c WKM Benjamin	b Walsh	6
AR Caddick	c Lara	b Walsh	1
ARC Fraser	not out		0
Extras	(lb 6, nb 1)		7
Total	(all out, 19.1 overs)		46

FoW: 1-0, 2-1, 3-5, 4-21, 5-26,
6-27, 7-37, 8-40, 9-45, 10-46.

Bowling	O	M	R	W
Ambrose	10	1	24	6
Walsh	9.1	1	16	3

The Wisden Trophy, 1993/94, 4th Test

West Indies v England

Kensington Oval, Bridgetown, Barbados
8, 9, 10, 12, 13 April 1994 (5-day match)

Result: England won by 208 runs
West Indies leads the 5-Test series 3-1

Toss: West Indies
Umpires: LH Barker and DB Hair (Aus)
Match Referee: JR Reid (NZ)
Man of the Match: AJ Stewart

Close of Play:

Day 1:   England 299/5 (Hick 26, Russell 3)
Day 2:   England 355, West Indies 188/7 (Chanderpaul
         31, Ambrose 35)
Day 3:   West Indies 304, England 171/3 (Stewart 62,
         Hick)

Day 4: England 394/7d, West Indies 47/2 (Lara 10, Arthurton 0)

England and 1ˢᵗ innings

Ma Atherton	c Lara	b KCG Benjamin	85
AJ Stewart		b WKM Benjamin	118
MR Ramprakash	c Murray	b WKM Benjamin	20
RA Smith	c Murray	b WKM Benjamin	10
GA Hick	c Murray	b Ambrose	34
GP Thorpe	c sub	b KCG Benjamin	7
RC Russell	c Chanderpaul	b Ambrose	38
CC Lewis	c Murray	b Ambrose	0
AR Caddick	b Ambrose		8
ARC Fraser	c Chanderpaul	b Walsh	3
PCR Tufnell	not out		0
Extras	(lb 8, nb 24)		32
Total	(all out, 100.2 overs)		355

FoW: 1-171, 2-223, 3-242, 4-265, 5-290
6-307, 7-307, 8-327, 9-351, 10-355.

Bowling	O	M	R	W
Ambrose	24.2	5	86	4
Walsh	24	3	88	1
WKM Benjamin	22	4	76	3
KCG Benjamin	20	5	74	2
Chanderpaul	10	4	23	0

West Indies 1st innings

DL Haynes	c Atherton	b Fraser	35
RB Richardson	c Atherton	b Fraser	20
BC Lara	c sub	b Lewis	26
KLT Arthurton	c Russell	b Fraser	0
JC Adams	c Thorpe	b Fraser	26
S Chanderpaul	c Ramprakash	b Tufnell	77
JR Murray	c Thorpe	b Fraser	0
WKM Benjamin	c Hick	b Fraser	8
CEL Ambrose	c Hick	b Fraser	44
KCG Benjamin	not out		43
CA Walsh	c Tufnell	b Fraser	13
Extras	(lb 1, nb 11)		12
Total	(all out, 101.5 overs)		394

FoW: 1-55, 2-55, 3-95, 4-126, 5-126,
6-126, 7-134, 8-205, 9-263, 10-304.

Bowling	O	M	R	W
Fraser	28.5	7	75	8
Caddick	24	2	92	0
Lewis	17	2	60	1
Tufnell	32	12	76	1

England and 2nd innings

MA Atherton	c Lara	b Walsh	15
AJ Stewart	b Walsh		143
MR Ramprakash	c Chanderpaul	b Walsh	3
RA Smith	lbw	b KCG Benjamin	13
GA Hick	c Lara	b Walsh	59
GP Thorpe	c Arthurton	b Walsh	84
RC Russell	not out		17
CC Lewis	c Walsh	b Adams	10
Extras	(b 8, lb 6, nb 36)		50
Total	(7 wickets declared, 108.5 overs)		394

DNB: AR Caddick, ARC Fraser, PCR Tufnell.

FoW: 1-33, 2-43, 3-79, 4-194, 5-344,
        6-382, 7-394

Bowling	O	M	R	W
Ambrose	22	4	75	0
Walsh	28	5	94	5
WKM Benjamin	22	3	58	0
KCG Benjamin	20	1	92	1
Chanderpaul	10	3	30	0
Adams	6.5	0	31	1

West Indies 2nd innings (target: 446 runs)

RB Richardson	c Ramprakash	b Caddick	33
JC Adams	c Russell	b Caddick	12
BC Lara	c Tufnell	b Caddick	64
KCG Benjamin	c Hick	b Caddick	0
KLT Arthurton		b Tufnell	52
S Chanderpaul	c sub (N Hussain)	b Hick	5
JR Murray	c Thorpe	b Caddick	5
DL Haynes	c Thorpe	b Tufnell	15
WKM Benjamin	c Stewart	b Tufnell	3
CEL Ambrose	b Lewis		12
CA Walsh	not out		18
Extras	(b 1, lb 7, nb 10)		18
Total	(all out, 82.2 overs)		237

FoW: 1-43, 2-43, 3-128, 4-150, 5-164,
6-179, 7-195, 8-199, 9-216, 10-237.

Bowling	O	M	R	W
Fraser	17	7	40	0
Caddick	17	3	63	5
Tufnell	36	12	100	3
Lewis	8.2	1	23	1
Hick	4	2	3	1

Day 2   DL Haynes (1) retired hurt on 35 from 51/0 to
126/4 (cut finger)

The Wisden Trophy, 1993/94 5th Test

West Indies v England

Antigua Recreation Ground, St John's Antigua
16, 17, 18, 20, 21 April 1994 (5-day match)

Result: Match drawn
West Indies wins the 5-Test series 3-1

Toss:	West Indies
Umpires:	S A Bucknor and DB Hair (Aus)
Match Referee:	JR Reid (NZ)
Test Debuts:	SC Williams (WI)
Man of the Match:	BC Lara
Man of the Series:	CEL Ambrose

Close of Play:
Day 1:   West Indies 274/3 (Lara 164, Arthurton 25)
Day 2:   West Indies 502/4 (Lara 320, Chanderpaul 41)
Day 3:   West Indies 593/5d, England 185/2 (Atherton
           63,   Smith 68)
Day 4:   England 442/6 (Russell 18, Lewis 12)

West Indies 1st innings

PV Simmons	lbw	b Caddick	8
SC Williams	c Caddick	b Fraser	3
BC Lara	c Russell	b Caddick	375
JC Adams	c sub	b Fraser	59
	(N Hussain)		
KLT Arthurton	c Russell	b Caddick	47
S Chanderpaul	not out		75
Extras	(lb 3, nb 23)		26
Total	(5 wickets declared, 180.2 overs)		

DNB: JR Murray, WKM Benjamin, CEL Ambrose, KCG Benjamin, CA Walsh.

FoW: 1-11 (Williams), 2-12 (Simmons), 3-191 (Adams), 4-374 (Arthurton), 5-593 (Lara).

Bowling	O	M	R	W
Fraser	43	4	121	2
Caddick	47.2	8	158	3
Tufnell	39	8	110	0
Lewis	33	1	140	0
Hick	18	3	61	0

England 1st innings

MA Atherton	c Murray	b Ambrose	135
AJ Stewart	c Ambrose	b KCG Benjamin	
			24
MR Ramprakash	lbw	b KCG Benjamin	
			19

RA Smith	lbw	b KCG Benjamin	175
GA Hick		b KCG Benjamin	20
GP Thorpe	c Adams	b Chanderpaul	9
+RC Russell	c Murray	b WKM Benjamin	62
CC Lewis	not out		75
AR Caddick	c WKM Benjamin	b Adams	22
ARC Fraser	b Adams		0
PCR Tufnell	lbw	b WKM Benjamin	0
Extras	(b 9, lb 20, nb 23)		52
Total	(all out, 106.1 overs)		593

FoW: 1-40, 2-70, 3-373, 4-393, 5-401,
             6-417, 7-535, 9-589, 10-593.

Bowling	O	M	R	W
Ambrose	40	18	66	1
Walsh	40	9	123	0
WKM Benjamin	41.1	15	93	2
KCG Benjamin	37	7	110	4
Chanderpaul	24	1	94	1
Adams	22	4	74	2
Athurton	2	1	4	0

West Indies 2nd innings

PV Simmons	not out	22
SC Williams	not out	21
Extras		0
Total	(o wickets, 24 overs)	43

DNB: BC Lara, JC Adams, KLT Arthurton, S Chanderpaul, JR Murray, WKM Benjamin, CEL Ambrose, KCG Benjamin, CA Walsh.

Bowling	O	M	R	W
Fraser	2	1	2	0
Caddick	2	1	11	0
Tufnell	6	4	5	0
Hick	8	2	11	0
Ramprakash	3	1	5	0
Thorpe	2	1	1	0
Stewart	1	0	8	0

JC Adams: 59 runs, 164 balls, 247 min. Dropped at 26 by Hick

BC Lara: 50 in 121 balls, 154 minutes, 7 fours 100 in 180 balls, 232 minutes, 16 fours 150 in 240 balls, 327 minutes, 22 fours 200 in 311 balls, 440 minutes, 27 fours 250 in 377 balls, 515 minutes, 32 fours 300 in 432 balls, 610 minutes, 38 fours 350 in 511 balls, 721 minutes, 42 fours 375 in 538 balls, 766 minutes, 45 fours

The highest test innings in history.

WI 500 runs in 673 min.

RA Smith: 175 runs, 418 min., 315 balls, 26x4, 3x6

MA Atherton: 135 runs, 539 min., 383 balls, 13x4

The third wicket partnership of 303 between Atherton and Smith was a record for that wicket for England against the West Indies.